Masterfully Broken Part 1

Masterfully Broken Part 1

Eugene Early

Cover Art by: Phokiis Summerz IG: neverlosephokiis
Copyright © 2024 by Eugene Early
All rights reserved. No part of this book may be reproduced in any manner whatsoever without written permission except in the case of brief quotations embodied in critical articles and reviews.
First Printing, 2024

Introduction

One day about a decade ago I sat alone in a small trailer in southeast Georgia thinking about my countless sexual experiences. I wondered how many women have I actually been with so I decided to count. Since I've been to a couple states I made a column for each state and started listing names. It wasn't long before I realized I didn't remember many names, my list started consisting of "ugly chick #1 & fat chick #2" & I almost immediately felt shame. I went over the list a few times because I couldn't believe what I was looking at, over 250 names I felt sick to my stomach and I decided to end my count. I wondered how did I have enough time to do this much fucking. How did I get this many women to give themselves to me? My self-esteem was low, I didn't feel like I had any "game", I wasn't some heartthrob that had women drooled over. "What the fuck was I doing?"

So I began to think about what satisfaction I gained from those experiences and why I sought them. This led me to some pretty interesting answers that reached back into my childhood. I think the general consensus on men dealing with a lot of women is that we're just immature and can't control ourselves. While not completely dismissing that because there are no absolutes I urge anyone reading this book to dig a little deeper. Men are humans with emotions too, we are effected subconsciously just like any other living being. Most of us may not realize it because we weren't raised to dig deep into our emotions or we just accept that being with multiple women is just part of being a man. During my soul searching I realized how much the relationship with my mother and early interactions with females shaped my views on women. I started understanding how my insecurities came about and how I coped with them.

This book isn't to glorify sleeping with a lot of women but to give insight on my experience and things that should be considered in general because I'm sure I'm not alone in my actions or thoughts. I procrastinated for years about writing this book because I wasn't ready to be completely honest, I was ashamed. Now I know that everything happens for a reason and these experiences were necessary to shape the man I am today. Some may read this and think I'm a disgusting pig others may respect my honesty. Either way I respect everyone's opinion, I'm a fan of the truth no matter how ugly or uncomfortable. I would say don't have any preconceive notions but I'm sure the title warrants them. Don't worry there will be some scandalous sex stories but I'm definitely putting medicine in the candy.

I urge men who read this book to look within themselves if they have some shady behavior that they may have let go unchecked and look for the source. It's a liberating thing to know why you're doing something and making the conscious decision of whether or not to continue. Also we need to be fair to women by not letting our subconscious damage cause emotional and physical harm to them. I want women who read this to come away with context and compassion for men and our behavior. Not saying you have to put up with bad behavior but a little understanding and compassion can go a long way. We aren't just dogs trying to get a bone, there's a reason for everything and it isn't so simple. Don't just write us off as being childish men who can't control our hormones. So please read with an open mind and enjoy.

Nobody's Baby Mama's Maybe

One of my earliest memories were when my mother, little sister and I moved to Baltimore. I'm not sure where my big brother was but I remember the three of us huddled up in the living room of a cold house with no electricity or furniture until the next day. My mother used the little change she had to buy a small cup of coffee and a hotdog from a 7-11 gas station down the street. She broke the hotdog into two pieces, one for my one year old sister and one for me and we all sipped the coffee. I knew my mother was hungry but she sacrificed so that we would have something in our stomachs. That's my first memorable experience of a mother's love and I made sure to tell her every day that I loved her, accompanied with a hug was my everyday routine for a few years. My grandmother gave me the same feeling, I remember hiding under her hospital bed that sat in our living room coincidentally the same spot where my mother held my sister and I when we first moved in. She was on hospice which I didn't know at the time because I was only 4 or 5 years old.

All I knew was I could run to that bed, and she would ward off my little sister and older brother who were picking on me, normal middle child issues I guess. I can't remember what she looked like, but I remember her presence. I remember feeling safe & warm knowing she had my back even though I was in no real danger, back then it felt like it to me. That comfort and security didn't last long unfortunately, I'll never forget the day she died. All the children in the family went to a block party a few blocks away and came back to my grandmother being loaded into an ambulance. I remember seeing her old, crusty feet on the gurney and feeling completely numb. I immediately felt guilty because while I was enjoying myself at a block party my grandmother was dying. Now I know there wasn't really anything that I could've done but it still hurt nonetheless. I don't remember crying or any sound for that matter, I just felt a sense of loneliness. I still had my mother though and I knew she would be there for me, at least that's what I thought back then.

A few years after my grandmother died, I remember going up to my mother for my routine "I love you" and hug only this time it was met with a "Boy get off me" and a push. In hindsight I understand she was frustrated about something else and didn't mean to hurt my feelings but at the time it crushed me. I didn't curse her in my head or anything, but I just thought to myself that I would never tell her that I loved her or hug her again. My mother was a product of her environment, crack hit the black community hard but in the northern city atmosphere it was brutal; I could tell that at an early age. Fortunately, she didn't parade men in and out the house, when we had one. Not sure if it was her struggling as a single mother or her crack addiction that often left us living in the basement of my aunt's house. It felt like living as a second-class citizen because my aunt had issues of her own. Getting drunk was an early sign that somebody in the house would surely be verbally or physically abused. She ran the show; everybody listened to her and had her to answer to including my uncle. If he would disagree with something or get out of line she would put him out and this was a routine, so I learned early that women ran the show.

My mother had a boyfriend that was a complete weirdo, he was quiet & awkward. He lived with us along with a family friend & his son, they slept in our living room. All I know is one day dude was sleeping on our couch while her boyfriend was upstairs and then the next day her boyfriend was out, and dude moved upstairs & in my mother's bed. I'm chuckling thinking about it now because he's my father and has been my father for over 25 years now but back then I thought "that's fucked up". Mama was still mama though I didn't look at her as a bad person. The beginning of their relationship was rocky to say the least, a lot of fights both physical and verbal. One argument in particular really stuck with me and confirmed my feeling of being alone and unprotected. They got into a routine argument one day and my mother just left my sister & I alone with her new, angry boyfriend. In his rage he spat on my sister as he walked past her and went downstairs. I angrily ran to the top of the stairs & yelled out to him "don't spit on my sister" he responded by running back upstairs to choke me out. Not sure if I passed out or the adrenaline from the situation caused my memory to be cloudy but I don't remember what happened immediately after that. All I know is my mother came back maybe a few minutes later and they stayed together.

Of course, he was the villain in my mind, but she was also his sidekick. I wondered "how valuable were we really to her?", the fact that she could up and leave her children with a violent man in the midst of a fight left me again with a feeling of being alone and unprotected. Not only that but I wondered who was really in charge, up until that point I had only seen women running things. Now my mother still pretty much ran the household but now there was someone she had to answer to before making any promises to us. It was both comforting and uncomfortable seeing my mother being submissive. He worked; she didn't so we got by on his paychecks and her welfare. He pretty much worked & slept, she handled the money and everything else. O yea and he got the "Big piece of chicken", some may not know but for a long time the "big piece of chicken" symbolized the hierarchy in the black household. Black men didn't get much recognition out in the world so the least his family could do was make sure he ate the best of what we had. As an added bonus he loved Captain Crunch, so he had his own box while we shared a generic bag of cereal which was fine, but he gave me something to strive for.

I wanted to have the proverbial "big piece of chicken" one day and have a woman that took care of home too. I didn't want the arguing and confrontation that came with their relationship though. Not sure what those were about but I know at the end of the day they had each other's back. The downside to those disagreements though were sometimes my mother would take her frustration out on us. Calling us "bitches" and other derogatory things that shouldn't be said to family especially children. So to combat that I stayed away from her as much as possible, I either played outside until she made us come in the house or I played quietly in my room. My mother ended up getting arrested but since her boyfriend was an orphan and he didn't want us to go into the system he married her. She was gone what seems like an eternity; in reality she was gone about a month. During that time he took care of us, he only knew how to fry chicken so that's pretty much all we ate the entire time. Even with the fights and foul things I've heard him say watching him take care of us when he was all we had gave me a newfound respect for him. My mother got out of jail and the 1st thing she offered to cook us was fried chicken to which we blurted out "Nooo."

Fast forward a few months some neighborhood bullies approached my little brother and I while we were playing with our wiffle ball bat set, they on the other hand had sticks and pipes. The main bully stepped up to me then turned to his friends to egg him on but in that moment I took my wiffle bat and hit him as hard as I could in his back. He dropped to his knees yelling; suddenly my mother called us in for dinner so I walked away. While eating my little brother told my mother I was about to fight. Her being who she was she ordered me to stop eating and go back outside to finish the fight. I went back outside and fought the boy, fortunately I won but I felt like an animal fighting while my mother and others stood around cheering. I wanted to confront the bully so I appreciated her letting me deal with it while there were adults around to make sure it was a fair fight, but it felt weird having my mother orchestrating that. She understood in the environment we were in that's how I had to be to give me a better chance at not only surviving but not being a victim so I'm grateful.

For a brief moment I somewhat became a bully, I got reprimanded often in elementary school for fighting girls. They would tease or say something I didn't like, and I would put them in a headlock or throw them around a little bit. I didn't like to fight but something about a female talking to me in a negative way didn't sit well with me, especially since I had to put up with it at home. Luckily, I had a male teacher who really got on me about fighting girls, he called me a coward and said I wouldn't do boys like that. So that no non-sense rule I had for girls I applied to everybody, and I started beating boys up. Once that happened that teacher started calling me "Bruiser". Once I felt like I got his respect and he didn't see me as a coward I did my best to stay out of fighting situations. I had already established myself in the neighborhood/school anyway so the other kids knew I wasn't a pushover. Moving around a lot this was routine, I was used to being the new kid on the block and having to fight because in that environment kids would pick a fight to make sure you weren't a punk.

The summer before my 12th birthday my life would be turned upside down; I learned some valuable lessons but it was definitely painful. We were living in east Baltimore at the time, one of only a few habitable houses on the block. My parents got news that my father's friend just passed away so they went to another friend's house I guess to mourn with other friends. This was in between my mother getting her welfare check and food stamps so there wasn't any food in the house. Around dinnertime the first night I called my mother telling her my little brother, sister & I were hungry. She rambled a little and told me she would be home soon; at that point I knew they were getting high so we were "shit out of luck" as she would say. So I made us some ketchup sandwiches and called it a night. Now when I woke up the next morning and they still weren't home

I got alarmed because they never stayed away that long before so I called again. She said she would be home soon and every call after that went unanswered.

We had enough bread for 2 more ketchup sandwiches so like I learned from my mother I made them for my little brother & sister, I didn't eat anything. By the time dinner came around my siblings were crying to me about being hungry and there was nothing I could do, hell I was hungry too. We all cried ourselves to sleep that night, I couldn't believe how they could leave us to starve basically just to get high; they'll be home tomorrow I thought. Tomorrow came and still now parents and no answered phone calls. At this point I'm starving and my siblings are hungry too. Now the rule was when they weren't there we couldn't leave the house but at this point we've been stuck in the house for three days. Our only neighbor was "Mr. John" him and his wife were nice people so I broke the rule and went to ask them if they had some food.

In that situation they were supposed to call child protective services and they even mentioned it but they asked me if I knew how to cook to which I replied "yes". Of course I didn't really know how to cook but my stomach told me I could figure it out. They gave me a tray of drum sticks and told me to come back if we needed anything else to eat. I took them home, fried them up using the steps I watched my mother use and just like that we're motherless feasting on fried chicken again. It was a bittersweet feeling; I was happy to finally eat but sad because my mother abandoned us for so long and wouldn't even answer the phone. "At least when they get here we can really eat well because the food stamps have been loaded onto her card",

I thought; boy was I wrong. When they came home a day or so later she told me the food stamps and her cash were gone. That was a crushing feeling and I knew our only alternative like we have done before was go to soup kitchens and church giveaways to eat and collect whatever food items they were giving away. I resented her for what she put us through, my father was there too but I didn't expect much from him. My mother on the other hand I expected that she would at least make sure we were fed. That woman who made sure we ate at her own expense was gone, this woman on the other hand didn't care if we starved as long as she could hit the pipe.

Soon after that my aunt moved onto the street behind us and our backyards actually faced each other. One day during a gathering I was chilling at home with my father watching westerns trying to figure out why he finds them so interesting. I wanted to ask my mother something so I went over to my aunt's house, couldn't find her anywhere. I came up to a female cousin's bedroom door where she appeared to be standing guard, "where's mommy?" I asked to which she replied "she's busy" with a smirk on her face. I walked away and waiting for my cousin to leave and I went back to her door knocking and calling my mother; "Give me a minute" she uttered. I went back to playing with the other kids and I overheard somebody say she was in the room with one of my cousin's friends. In that moment I felt anger and humiliation because at this point I had a pretty good idea of what they were doing and everybody knew it. In my mind that was an act of treason so I had to go tell my father.

I got back home and ran right to my father and told him she was held up in a room with some dude and wouldn't open the door when I was trying to talk to her. The look in his eyes were pure shock but he didn't go over there, I'm sure he understood he was outnumbered. I don't know what my parents next interaction was but soon after we were moving back into my aunt's house and she told everyone that I told my father. "How could you rat on your own mother?" my aunt yelled in front of all my cousins, of course there wasn't anything I could say. I don't remember my mother being angry at me but things felt different. In my mind though she was still a traitor, my father technically my stepfather had been the most consistent person I've ever seen and he took care of us not just financially but when my mother was in jail. Ironically it was this very same aunt who put her there but that's another story. This was right at the beginning of summer so luckily I didn't have to go to school.

That summer would be a pivotal moment in my life that in its negativity would bloom some positive things that would essentially save my life. I started that summer taking a sip of my older cousin's alcohol and a puff of his cigarettes here and there. As you could imagine marijuana was next. I didn't have any friends or any male relatives around my age so I hung with the older guys. From strong arm robbery to burglary they dabbled in it all and I was right there with them being a look out and assisting in whatever way I could. With the little money they gave me here and there I bought my own weed, cigarettes and alcohol. I thought it was cool back then; the Asian liquor store owners had no problem selling me anything I had the money for. Here I am a 12-year-old going to the liquor store buying alcohol and cigarettes subconsciously wanting somebody to stop me. When my mother found out I was smoking and drinking she didn't attempt to stop me at all, she just said she'd rather I do it around her than strangers. I definitely resented her for that but the things that would happen next absolutely disgusted and infuriated me.

Her boyfriend who was around 22 years old at the time was pretty much the ring leader of most of the dumb shit we were getting into. He was childish of course at 22 and would do things to antagonize me. My birthday was coming up in august and my mother promised me she would get me 2 pair of shoes and 2 outfits when she got her welfare check that month. That was huge for me because at the time I wore a size 13 shoe and I definitely wore adult clothing because I've always been big for my age. Outside of school uniforms my clothes came from church or shelter giveaways. So the day she got her check I'm outside bragging to everybody about how I'm getting some new shoes when her boyfriend walked up and told me to shut up or I wouldn't get anything. "I'm getting my stuff" I retorted, he just walked into the house and went to the basement where my mother was. I waited about 30minutes or so until he left and I went down to see my mother and ask when where we going to the store. She told me she had no money and she would make it up to me at Christmas, she had given him all her money. That crushed me because that was the only thing I had to look forward to. I was already wearing a pair of my cousin's size 10 shoes so I really needed some shoes and whatever this dude told her was more important to her than my aching feet.

So at that point I really felt like no one cared about me and I was on my own but I still hung around the older guys because I was trying to fit in. Shortly after that my mother came in the house bleeding saying my father had cut her arm. My family went into a frenzy screaming about what they were going to do to him and I can remember thinking "that's just what your ass get". I wasn't angry at him at all, I actually felt sorry for him. I saw how my mother's actions affected him, eyes bloodshot red, crying, getting high; he was going through it and it was all because of her. I wondered were all females this damn evil; even my little sister started showing signs of crazy. She tried to cut me with a bottle when I told her not to hang around certain people. I wanted to be that voice of reason to her that I didn't have but my voice of reason was drowned out by everybody else condoning the behavior just like they did me. In that experience however I got a good look at a life I didn't want for myself or my children, I didn't know how but I knew It wouldn't be my destiny.

Feeling guilty her boyfriend gave me a pair of his old low cut Timberland boots because we wore the same size. Here I am wearing a pair of boots in the summer but at least my feet didn't hurt anymore. That would be short lived because one late night he and others thought it would be funny to strip me outside. I was able to pick up one boot to cover my private area as I ran around the block through the alley to get into the house because they locked the front door. They came in laughing and I found out that he threw the other boot down into the sewer so back into my cousin's size 10s I go. That combined with them telling me if we ever got caught with anything

I should take responsibility because I was a minor led me to not really fuck with them much. I tried to stay to myself as much as possible in that crowed house.

My mother got back with my father at the end of the summer. I was confused to why he took her back. I saw him as being weak, I was grateful but I still felt like what she did was so horrible it shouldn't be forgiven. Luckily for me he didn't feel the same, she was a different person around him as opposed to my family. Maybe that was just a phase but it still damaged my relationship with her. I always heard women including her saying they'd never choose a man over their children but I learned the hard way that it's not always the case. There were many experiences that caused disdain for my mother but the couple I mentioned were the biggest ones that took away a lot of respect I had for her. She never came to any PTA meetings or checked my homework. Her thing was she didn't care if I went to school but I had to be out of the house during school hours. A part of me felt like I wouldn't live to see 18 years old anyway so I didn't have a plan but I still went to school because I knew the street life wasn't for me. Once she got back with my father my marijuana usage slowed down dramatically till I stopped completely. Getting high by myself made me feel lame and I asked myself why even do this shit at all.

After that things were pretty much on autopilot at home, I went to school stayed out of my mother's way as much as possible. I say my mother's way because my father wasn't a factor outside of distributing the more serious ass whippings, he pretty much worked and slept. There were the occasional mishaps where we would forget to clean something properly or break something. At that point we would be called "Trifling bitches" and a slew of other epithets, it was hurtful for a while but I became numb to the verbal abuse or at least I thought. School was really boring to me so I started cutting classes, rushing through my work so I could play classroom games with other kids or simply stare off thinking about a better life. One day a teacher kicked me out, she was an old black woman with similar mannerisms of my mother. I left the classroom & forgot my notebook so as I'm walking back up to the classroom door she comes out with it but tells me to ask for it politely. Here I am with uncontrollable testosterone running through my puberty riddled body feeling challenged or yet again by another female.

Before I could consider the repercussions, I lunged at her and snatched my notebook from her hands. Now this level of aggression from a black male is never tolerated in society no matter what his emotional or mental state is. So the school police officer took me to his office until my mother could come get me, I'm grateful he didn't take me to jail. He was a black man and considering the talk we had he empathized with my experience. On the other hand my heart was racing because I knew my mother was going to whip my ass. She barely left the house for anything and we didn't have a car so she had to catch buses to come get me.

She arrived with an irritated look on her face but she listened to my side of the story and told me I had to accept whatever consequences came with my actions. I've been suspended before so no problem or so I thought. My punishment while on suspension from school was I couldn't go outside which I really didn't play outside anyway so I wasn't hurt by that. Half way through my suspension though we were informed that the teacher was pressing charges against me for assault. Now I'm consumed by fear but my mother was definitely my rock in that situation because she never panicked or got overly emotional. She was with me every step of that process, obviously I was a minor so she had to be but I felt her support. She didn't hold my hand she stayed behind me and had me communicate with my public defender yet I knew if I needed her she'd step in. My teacher wanted an apology to drop the charge so I did and that was the end of that. I understood she wanted me to show respect but I felt like she could've talked to me instead of bringing me into court. I was just glad it was over but missing so much school caused me fail the 8th grade. I thought about quitting school, I didn't want to endure the embarrassment of going to school with kids a year younger than me. At that point no one else in my family to my knowledge graduated High School so I figured no big deal. My mother however assured me I could finish. Besides just laying up in her house was out of the question so I knew if I did drop out the streets would be my only option and my adolescent years taught me the streets were not for me.

I swallowed my pride and went back to school for my second 8th grade year. My high school years were much smoother for the most part. I still hadn't lost my virginity mainly because I didn't attempt to talk to girls because I thought they were inherently evil. I mean most of the females I'd encountered where abusing me verbally, emotionally or physically. I feared rejection so to save myself embarrassment I stayed away. Secondly I hadn't been circumcised and I overheard some neighborhood girls laughing about "ant-eaters" so my confidence was shot. Finally it occurred to me that I should lie to my doctor and tell him it was bothering me so he could do the circumcision. It worked & I got it done, I remember thinking on my ride back from the hospital "I'm ready to fuck something". Until I unwrapped my dick for the 1st time and it looked like a deformed pencil. Not girth wise but the head was abnormally pointed with stitches all around it. "WHAT THE FUCK HAVE I DONE" was the only thing running through my head as my heart pounded. Next was "there's no way this shit going to look normal once it heals", boy was I wrong luckily.

From about age 8 I was a chronic masturbator, going at it almost every day. Now at age 17 I couldn't touch my tool for 4-6 weeks. That was hell on a teenage virgin and I had an accident. I woke up around 3am one morning to one of those softcore HBO pornos and before I could get to the remote my little big guy started swelling. Next thing I know I popped a stitch and blood starts leaking out of my dick & I'm panicking. Not much because the healing was almost complete so I stopped the blood and it was fine.

Fast-Forward to spring break I reconnect with an old classmate from elementary school on a dating chatroom. For 3 days straight we rode the bus to a mall and I took her to see a movie. I liked the feeling of being cuddled up with a girl, getting my feel on slightly here and there. I didn't have the courage to make any overt moves though and I guess she got tired of waiting. We were in my room in the basement after seeing a movie when she asked me "Can I seduce you", nervously I uttered "yeah" not knowing what to expect. She pulls my dick out and starts sucking like a pornstar, I went into a frenzy damn near a seizure. My head was sensitive because it had been covered for most of my life so that sensation was overwhelming but in a good way. I'm thinking to myself "This is not a drill nigga you prepared for this moment" so I grab a red lifestyle condom I had gotten for free from the school nurse and tried to put it on. Nobody told me there were different condom sizes, that condom was so tight when I finally got it on. I kept going limp because it was cutting off my circulation but I managed to stay up enough to satisfy her. Immediately after we finished my little cousin opens the basement door and comes down to see us laying naked; he ran up to the kitchen to tell my mother. She didn't say anything but paranoid we got dressed, she did the "walk of shame" and I waited with her at the bus stop until her bus came. I get back in the house to my mother still cooking and she says "I'm glad you got some I thought you were gay" and everybody burst out laughing.

As you can imagine after that I walked around with my head held high or as my mother would say I was "smelling myself". I started talking back or just overall rejecting the verbal abuse I grew accustomed to taking. One day she said something that hurt my feelings so I blurted out "you aren't raising us welfare is" to which she responded by hitting me repeatedly with a broomstick. After about the 2 or 3rd swing I grabbed it and pushed it and her away from me as I ran down the stairs to the 1st floor. As I walked back to the basement door I heard "I should've swallowed you" followed by a skillet to the back of my head. I just kept going to my room, she didn't follow me down there. Things cooled down and by the time I came up for dinner she was cooking dinner with the lopsided skillet she had just hit me with. Every time I saw it I would have no choice but to think about how the dent got there. The quagmire here is at what point if any is it appropriate for a child to defend themselves from a parent? Or are they supposed to take the abuse and say "yes ma'am, no ma'am?" The shock on my mother's face when I grabbed the broomstick said "how dare you defend yourself" which made her angrier. It could have very well been that I reminded her of my father.

My biological father from what I'm told was an evil bastard, he supposedly pistol whipped my when I was a few months old in a heated argument with my mother. He was verbally and physically abusive, so much so my grandmother came over with a pistol to run him off and he never came back. After witnessing the treachery in my family and the unflattering behavior of my mother I often wondered if he was really as bad as they said he was. Like me he could have gotten tired of the verbal or physical abuse and lashed out our maybe not but I'll never know. What I do know is that a woman's words hold the power to build a man up or tear him down. Now on the surface you might think I'm bashing my mother when I should be bashing my father because he wasn't around. Truth is I'm not trying to bash anyone, I understand I come from a damaged people and my parents did the best they could with what they had. It took a while to get to that thought process because I had to experience life to understand other angles of the same reality.

Even though I didn't get the masculine energy I needed from my father or a male figure I think I would've been alright with the divine feminine energy from my mother. Unfortunately she raised me from a masculine space which didn't sit well with me. Boys need discipline and structure from masculine men, we can respect that from a male. Have you ever wondered how men raised by women could grow up to be abusers of women or just have little to no respect for them? From my own experience and observation I think when we get masculine energy from a feminine body we reject and resent it. I couldn't fight my mother but lashed out at girls in my school when I felt disrespected by them. I respected verbal discipline from my male teachers but felt challenged and disrespected when female teachers would chastise me. This is in no way trying to bash women I just think there's plenty of conversation around men and what we need to do better which is needed but not enough around what women can do to improve. I understand women do the best they can but like the saying says "with great power comes great responsibility". Women are the nation builders, our 1st teachers, our nurturers so when all else fails we need you to be fully grounded in your essence. My advice for women would be to dig into your feminine essence and stay there, that's more than enough to give your child what they need to grow up a decent human being. However when you try to be the "mother and the father" there's going to be a severe imbalance that will have long term effects as we're seeing now in today's society.

Even lead by example, a lot of times we hear how no good women are from our mothers and other women. If you don't want to hang around or cooperate with other women why should we? More than what you say kids watch what you do. Watching women in my family gave me a very traumatic view of what women are. I heard the phase "Mama's baby daddy's maybe" when I was a kid and I vilified my biological father for not being around which could be warranted. As I got older though I wondered; whose baby was I really? I didn't feel secured in anyone's heart, my mother's sometimes. Nobody's baby, Mama's maybe?

Genesis

After high school I started working at McDonalds trying to figure out what I was going to do next. I thought I wouldn't live long enough to graduate but here I am a high school graduate with no solid plans for the future. After a few months of working fast food I decided I would try to join the police department. Coincidentally the Baltimore City Police department had a cadet program hiring event coming up so I went and got rejected because I smoked marijuana a few months earlier on prom night. So now I'm really just lost so I started chasing the only thing that made me feel accomplished; PUSSY!!!! Back then we didn't have social media as we now know it; we had chat rooms. Boost mobile was popular then so I hopped on their chat room "Boost Hookt". I met up with a couple women and knocked 'em down, one I called "Twin Towers" on account of her huge titties. 50DDD if I remember correctly, I was 19 and she was 36 living in her friends living room so it was a dusty situation but I was young chasing a nut. I didn't run any kind of games back then I just would be myself and pussy would just fall into my lap. It wouldn't be too long after that I would meet a woman that would deliver the death blow to the little innocence I had left.

Her name was Rochelle, we met on Boost Hookt and she invited me over to her house one afternoon. She was laid back with pretty eyes and big titties, if you haven't figured it out yet I LOVE TITTIES!!!!!! She dressed like a tomboy, she had on camouflage pants and a plain black T-shirt. We sat around having general conversation and watching T.V. with 2 of her 5 children until she told me she had to go pick up her other kids from school; I offered to walk with her. We really hit it off and made plans to spend a night together a few days later. I came around 7pm to a full house, her sisters were over with their children so she told me I could go lay in her bed. I did and I felt her climb into bed and cuddle with me later that night. The next morning we lay in bed talking, she's naked and I'm just trying to keep my cool. Laying on her back she throws her legs over my waist and we're flirting and rubbing at this point, she tells me how wet she was. I began massaging her thigh, working my way up close to her pussy but her juices met me on her inner thigh before I could get there.

At that point I knew it was on so I pulled my dick out and started rubbing her clit with it till she raised her hips causing me to slide right in. She wasn't tight by a long shot but it was wet and her titties and eyes turned me on. That was the start of our "situationship", I pretty much moved in after that. It felt better than staying in the basement at my parent's house. She didn't clean, barely did any real cooking, sex and sympathy is what kept my immature dumbass around. Sexually she turned me out, she was the 1st woman to suck my toes and eat my ass. Yea I said it she ate my ass which I honestly didn't know was a thing until she told me to lay on my stomach one night. It felt gay and wrong after a few minutes so I would stop it but those 1st few minutes were amazing. All I knew was no women had ever made me feel that good and I wasn't going to let something like a dirty house stop me from getting all that, or so I thought.

After a couple months I started feeling cheated, I worked at McDonalds making $6.15 an hour then came home to clean and cook while she sat on her ass all day. I remember one argument like it was yesterday, I came home to find her kids eating uncooked noodles straight out the package for dinner. That pissed me off, I got on her about it and she argued and got a little physical pointing her finger in my face, chest bumping me and just being real aggressive so I left. This kind of shit happened ever so often and she would call me crying about how nobody else would want her because she had so many kids and she just wanted to talk. I would go over to her house, she would throw that pussy on me and I would be moving my couple bags of clothes and T.V. back over. This was absolutely a toxic relationship but where I came from it was relatively normal behavior. I also loved her children and wanted to be there for them because she wasn't taking care of them properly in my opinion. I didn't know it then but as I think back now she reminded me of my mother. Very aggressive in the way she talked to her kids, threatening them. I thought I could save them all, the irony is I didn't even know how to save myself.

Eventually I slipped up and I shot a huge load in her, I remember like it was yesterday. Her face covered in a creepy smirk which I thought was an accomplished smile in the moment but in retrospect it was an "I got you now muthafucka" smile. After that the sex started slowing up and her attitude got worse. My plan was to go to a junior college in New York and transfer to a D1 school to play football but she was insecure about me leaving and going that far. To compromise I decided to attend a local college which she had a problem with still. She felt like I would go to college and find someone my age with no kids and less baggage, she was absolutely correct but I didn't know that at the time. We argued about my college ambitions one day, I got pissed and stormed out of her house flipping a couch over along the way. I get half way down the block to realize I left my phone on the charger so I walk back to the house and as I'm approaching the front porch she comes out to snap my phone in half and throws it into the street. I'm furious at this point so I pick the 2 pieces of my phone up and walk onto her porch as she threatens to call the police on me. I told her go ahead I would break her phone after she made the call. I grabbed her phone and we tussled over it even falling into the living room window it didn't break but it was damaged. I finally got her phone and I snapped it in 2 like she did mine.

Now in my head I'm thinking If I leave it would be a warrant for my arrest and that's not good so I'll just wait here and tell my side of the story; man was I wrong. When the police arrived I sat on the front porch and started explaining what happened, they weren't trying to hear shit. They saw a 6'5" 280lbs young black man and a crying woman and children, o yea when they pulled up she pulled her acting skills out and started crying; naturally her kids would cry too once they saw her in distress. They told me they had to put me in zip tie cuffs till they got things figured out, I didn't get out of those things till I was at the station. Getting into that paddy wagon was the worst feeling of my life, I remember thinking I did all that shit as a juvenile; no arrest now here I am as an adult going to jail over a bitch. I felt like John Coffey from "The Green Mile", they had to connect 2 ankle cuffs together so I could be cuffed with my hands behind my back. They didn't empty my pockets at the police station so I got to the bottom half of my phone and desperation told me I could still dial somebody's number but I had no luck with that. From the police station they took me to central booking, sitting/laying cold in over-crowed cells for hours. I had to strip down to be searched, as I spread my ass cheeks and coughed I thought "I'm going to kill that bitch". I had never been that miserable before in my life and all I could think was "I've become a statistic".

The jailhouse lawyers kept telling me I would get out on my own recognizance because I didn't have a record. I thought seeing the bail commissioner would be in a court setting like the movies but we were led to some booths, there I got crushing news. My bail was set at $5,000; I couldn't get out on my own recon because I didn't have a steady address over the years. We got evicted & moved around a lot growing up so that came back to bite me in the ass even though I was a kid; it wasn't my fault. Since I couldn't pay bail I was moved upstairs to actual dorms/cell blocks whatever they're called. I felt like my life was over, the week I was arrested I was supposed to take my placement exam and file for financial aid. I stayed to myself and nobody bothered me so I wasn't scared of anyone in there it was more feeling like the world was passing me by that got to me. My arraignment was next and I was sure the judge would consider I have no criminal record, enrolled in college and let me out without bail. I stood as the judge read off my case, when she said I tried to push my PREGNANT girlfriend out of a window I almost passed out. I felt like everybody in the court side-eyed me and all I could do was give the judge a look to say "I didn't do that shit". It didn't matter my bail stayed the same which meant I was staying in there. I needed $500 to get out but to a family of broke crackheads who were barely making it as is that was almost impossible. Here I am my life ruined over a bad decision and $500 debt essentially.

Besides not getting out I learned in court that I was going to be a father, I was annoyed that she didn't tell me she was pregnant. After a few more days my mother told me that she and Rochelle had put their money together to pay a bail bondsman and I would be out soon. She also let me know that she going to be evicted so she was moving in with Rochelle. So the good news was I would be getting out of jail the bad news was that I would be getting out to homelessness. So when I get out I run straight to my "gangsta boo", I met her before Rochelle and I kept in touch with her. I call her my "gangsta boo" because she sold drugs among other things and she was tough. On the outside you would think she was a stud because she dressed like a guy and didn't have much of a feminine aura around her but she loved dick believe me. I told her about everything that happened and as you could imagine she wanted to fuck Rochelle up but she was pregnant with my child so I couldn't let that happen. I stayed with her for a night and went to my cousin's house the next day where I pretty much stayed for a while. Times when I didn't want to be in their crowded home I would sleep on a park bench or spend the night with a female. It was a pretty miserable time because I had a domestic violence charge lingering over my head and I knew I wouldn't take any kind of deal so it would be an uphill battle.

This 1 chick in particular stood out during this time; she was short, chubby and probably mixed with Puerto Rican or something. She delivered Chinese food at night so I would ride with her on deliveries some nights and she would pay me a couple dollars, sometimes we fucked after sometimes we didn't. After a while she mentioned being married but her husband was in the military and deployed overseas. Though she treated me good I definitely looked at her differently. I would still go to visit my parents and Rochelle to see how she was doing but I had to use the basement door. That speaks volumes of the kind of evil I was dealing with because that shit was petty. On Valentine's Day I used my little Chinese delivery money to buy her a little gift bag. When I gave it to her without any eye contact she literally threw it in a corner and all the little gifts went all over the place. Just like when I was a child with my mother I thought to myself "I'm never doing that shit for her again."

One night while riding around on food deliveries after reflecting on everything I closed my eyes, heart full of despair I said to myself "GOD deliver me from this crazy bitch." The next morning I got a call from her crying saying she lost the baby and she was in the hospital. I went to see her because that's the kind of person I am but man was I relieved. She cried in my arms when I got there and apologized; she asked if we could try again, in my head I'm thinking "Bitch is you crazy" but with my words I said "Just get better." She wanted to get back together and I was tired of sleeping on my cousin's couch and delivering food so I agreed. My 1st court date came up, I went alone and they offered me a "Stet" as they called it. They said the charges would be on hold for a year, if I didn't get arrested for the same thing it would go away but if I did I would be charged with both. Now that I knew what kind of evil I was dealing with I wasn't about to let a charge linger knowing she could call the police anytime and fuck my life up so I rejected the offer and got another court date. Another cousin of mine suggested I go into the marines so I went down to the recruiting station but at 6'5" 280lbs they told me I was too big and I quote "Try the Army" which I did.

My weight wasn't an issue with the army but my lingering domestic violence charge was, the recruiter told me If I had a domestic violence conviction I wouldn't be able to carry a firearm and therefore would disqualify me from joining. After telling Rochelle about this along with me telling her I wasn't going to accept these charges she agreed to go to my next court date and tell the truth. On court day as we're sitting in the courtroom the prosecutor comes in and says to everyone "Do you all know the judge can violate all of you, you're still not supposed to be around each other", instantly like musical chairs all the men got up and moved around to find another seat. At that moment I realized the dysfunction in most relationships in the environment I was in. When my case came up Rochelle stood up in court and said that everything was a lie and the charges were dropped. In my head I'm thinking her ass should be locked up but NOPE it's like the system was only interested in getting me into the mass incarceration machine. I was grateful though because now I could proceed with my enlistment into the Army. I was numb to a degree living with

Rochelle, I was pretty much walking on eggshells. I wasn't allowed to use the house phone, she wouldn't teach me how to drive; I pretty much was stuck in the house.

One day she gave me a ride to the Army recruiter's office and the recruiter opened his big mouth about how much more money we would get if we were married, I already knew that but I wasn't going to tell her that. From that point on she would make little comments about wanting to get married or that she wasn't important to me. I told her we could get married once I completed my training which was a lie, I planned on leaving and not looking back. My father who hadn't really given me any advice over the years looked at me one day and said "I know I've never really told you much before but DON'T MARRY THAT GIRL." My mother on the other hand thought marriage was the most admirable thing I could do, taking on the responsibility of being a father to those children. In reality I was still a kid myself but the feeling of being in an "already made family" gave me a sense of purpose. For whatever reason I couldn't tell you why but I agreed to get married and on April 1st 2008 we got married, YES I got married on April Fool's Day. 8 days later I left for basic training, only married a week and I was leaving for a few months but I felt confident everything would be ok.

Basic training was a culture shock for sure, being woken up to banging trash cans and yelling followed by hours of standing and waiting for different phases of being processed in. Even only a week in guys where calling home to other men answering their woman's phone or hearing from friends how their girl is fucking around already. I felt sorry for them but I thought "they shouldn't have married hoes" that would never happen to me. Having 5 children and living with my family there was no way my wife would do me like that. About a month past with only 1 letter from my wife and 1 package with all the wrong things that I told her wasn't allowed in basic training. I remember feeling like an orphan during mail call; everybody else getting multiple letters, none for me. A few people smuggled phones into our dorm and I used one of theirs routinely. As usual I sat on the floor next to my bed and called my mother at that point she started spilling the beans. She told me my wife had moved another woman in and was messing around with some young dude from the neighborhood. I tried to keep a straight face but my throat felt like it closed up on me I could barely breathe. A "battle buddy" walked up and asked me what was wrong and all I could say was "Jody struck again". Jody was the stereotypical name we used in the military for the guy who screws a soldier's woman.

As you can imagine I called my wife as soon as I could, I didn't scream at her I just asked what was going on. She denied everything and told me my family was just mad because she stopped giving them money. So I was torn between my wife and my family, I honestly didn't know who to believe because they all had done some pretty foul things to me. When I got married my mother told me to always put my wife 1st even before her, so that ran through my head constantly but I had a decision to make while still struggling to adjust and keep up in basic training. Similar to a scene in "Jarhead" I took the only letter I had from my wife in which she wrote some freaky things, I went into a bathroom stall to masturbate while reading the letter and thinking about her. It made me feel closer to her even though I was a thousand miles away. I was a teddy bear when I went into the Army but training turned me into a grizzly bear so I didn't have the same presence as I did before. Our next phone conversation I said "You're my wife, if you say you didn't do it I have to believe you but if I ever find out it's true no matter how much time has passed I'm going to hurt you." She replied "What if some of it's true", at that moment I knew everything was true and rage took over and we argued a little before I had to get off the phone.

After that we argued a few more times before she started calling my unit to tell them I wasn't taking care of my family. I got paid $1500 every 2 weeks to a joint account that she was the primary on, I would take out $400 for myself and she kept the other $1100; keep in mind she was on section-8 so she paid no rent, she got about $700 in food stamps and about the same in cash assistance. Needless to say she was living carefree financially while I went through the mental & emotional rollercoaster that came with army training. So a day after pay day a Drill Sergeant pulls me into his office to tell me my wife called again and that I had to send the money I withdrew back to her. Which meant I no longer had any money for toiletries, paid phone calls or any of the other few things we could spend our money on in training. I was infuriated that after all the effort I put into doing right by this woman she was out to hurt me in any way she could. The silver lining about my week in jail was my cellmate taught me how to make dice out of wet toilet paper so that's what I did and I earned money for my toiletries by shooting dice. Yea a soldier in Army basic training making

$3000 a month had to gamble in order to have soap to wash his ass.

Even through all of that I felt like getting a divorce was a failure that I wasn't willing to accept so I asked her to come see me during my graduation from basic training. I sent some of my dice money to her in addition to my paycheck so she wouldn't have an excuse not to come. I was definitely wrong on that assumption because she definitely didn't come and to make things worse I found out there would be no graduation for me because I failed my physical training test. I went to a fitness training unit where we exercised 3 times a day all week and a weekly P.T. test for a month, if we didn't pass by then we would be sent home. The night before my last test Rochelle and I had an emotional conversation and she told me she hopes I fail my test so I could come home to her. When we got off the phone I lay there thinking about what going back to her would mean. It would mean going back to being treated like a 2nd class citizen, back to depending on a woman who got me arrested for nothing, back to living my life on eggshells; no fucking way I was letting that happen. The morning came & I started my 6'5" 305lbs frame around the track on my 2 mile run that I needed to complete in 15 minutes and 56 seconds or less.

One mile in I could feel my asthma kicking in and it became harder to breathe, I took huge inhales through my nose and deep exhales out my mouth to help keep my airways open. The thought of how miserable the life I left was and how depressing it would be to go back, I barely made it out I knew I wouldn't survive if I had to go back. With a quarter mile left Rochelle's voice popped into my head "come back to me",

"HELL NO" I thought and with my airways barely open; I galloped across the finish line. 15:44 a Drill Sergeant yelled as I collapsed trying to relax so my airways could open back up. I had never felt that accomplished before in my life, after celebrating I ran straight to my phone to call Rochelle. "I'm never coming back BITCH!!!!!" I replied as soon as she answered the phone. Of course that started an argument but I wasn't angry I was relieved and felt like throwing my accomplishment in her face since she couldn't find it in her dark heart to encourage me to succeed. After my gloating I thought about who I could share the good news with my mind was completely blank and I realized I didn't have anyone. The little connection with my family wasn't strong because of the role they played in keeping my wife's infidelity a secret; I cried myself to sleep that night.

It would take another week for me to be processed out to my next training location so I hopped on another chatroom. I started talking to chick in her late 20's to early 30's I believe, she was cool easy to talk to and she was willing to meet. Now that I've complete my basic training obligation I had the freedom to move around base unsupervised, I took it upon myself to catch a cab off base though. I got a room at a motel not too far away and waited for her horny as hell, this had been the longest I've went without sex since I lost my virginity; it had been over 3 months. She called me to let me know she was almost there but she had to bring her children because she couldn't find a babysitter. I thought to myself "why the hell would she bring her kids when we're supposed to be fucking?" I just knew I wasn't getting any ass that day but I appreciated her coming to see me.

They finally arrived and I opened the door to a cute brown skinned bbw with a 2 year old boy and daughter a couple years older. They came in to cartoons playing on the television because I already knew something was needed to hold their attention while I talked and rubbed on their mama. The more I realized they weren't paying us any attention the more I started thinking I might be able to get some so I got under the covers and invited her to get under too; she did. We'd been doing so much rubbing pre-cum is oozing out my dick so I pulled it out and put her hand on it to which she responded by gripping it tight and started stroking it slowly. Shortly after she turns around and starts giving me head under the covers, the kids are still watching cartoons and playing around at the foot of the bed. It starts feeling so good that I forgot to keep a lookout and when I open my eyes her son was standing right next to the bed looking at me; I gave him a playful nudge and told him to keep playing and he did. Now in hindsight this was a very fucked up situation but my hormones didn't allow me to recognize that in the moment I could only think about the nut I would surely bust soon.

She turned onto her side and I slid into her from behind and maintained slow, deliberated strokes as to not rock the bed and break the concentration between the children and the cartoons they were watching. It didn't take long before I released inside of her and for a few minutes all the bullshit I had been going through was gone and was completely relaxed. After that shame set in when I realized I'd just fucked a chick in the same room as her children. "They're young they won't remember" I rationalized with myself to relieve my conscience. Back to base

I go because I wasn't allowed off in the 1st place, I let her keep the room for the night. It was already paid for and they all were tired from the ride earlier. Shortly after I left for my next training location in Alabama. At this point I wasn't excited about anything, the reason I joined the Army was no longer there. I only joined to support my wife and her children but I was almost certain we wouldn't be getting back together.

Alabama would be my next duty station for my specialty training which was ammunition but a few good things happened. Rochelle stood me up again so I decided that divorce was absolutely necessary, I found out I didn't have to pay her my whole check only a couple hundred dollars so that was a pleasant surprise. My mother started mailing me the divorce papers and I would complete them and mail back with the filing fee. Shortly after initiating my divorce I saw this gorgeous black woman working in the customer service department of the store on base. She was short maybe 5ft tall at the most, plus sized with a big ole booty and I had to have her. I would flirt with her whenever I came to the store, she told me I was too young for her but I wasn't about to let that stop me from trying. I was 20 and she was 29 I believe, her presence was graceful and soft; her voice even softer. I would bring her gift baskets every now and then and just talk to her while she worked and I had a little time to spare.

One day I guess my consistency paid off because she gave me her number and we started communicating. She had recently gone through a divorce so she could empathize with me and the process I was going through. I fell head over heels for her because her soft, nurturing spirit was just what I needed.

My nose was so open two weeks after we initially starting conversing over the phone I got her name tattooed on my chest. I just knew this would be my boo forever and I'm sure a piece of her thought I was crazy. Her divine feminine presence started repairing my wounded masculinity. I wasn't depressed anymore and all of a sudden I had things to look forward to. We went at it like rabbits and had lots of pillow talk and the things she went through made me want to take care of her.

My duty station changed after graduation and I would be going to Georgia and without much hesitation she quit her two jobs to move with me. I remember the complete feeling I felt loading up the moving truck with her car in tow. Riding down the highway with her in the passenger seat and her 4 month old son in his car seat in between us. Just like that I had a family again, stopping along the way for various things made me feel like one of those Disney movies I watched growing up of families taking road trips. We'd picked a duplex out of a newspaper because it fit our almost non-existent budget and the owner was willing to work with us on paying the deposit. When we got there the price made sense because that place was a shithole deep in the country, I was embarrassed. We had nowhere else to go so we were stuck with it and that made me feel like a failure, I failed her in my eyes. She left a pretty decent life to follow me and I led her into inferior living conditions.

After the initial disdain she tapped into that energy all women have and created an environment that was decent. She laid wallpaper on the crappy surfaces and decorated a little with the things she had bought and her willingness to start from the bottom with me made me appreciate her even more. That was short lived; I noticed after she got our place together she wouldn't do much but send me to the store for ice cream and sleep. "Damn she done changed up on me" I thought, this isn't the woman I knew who worked 2 jobs. I talked to my mother and explained everything and she said "she's nesting", as you can imagine I didn't know what that was. She explained to me that it's when pregnant women prepare their home for a new baby which blew my mind because pregnancy never crossed my mind. We were low on money but I kept getting cheap pregnancy tests from a dollar store and 8 tests later they all said negative. So now I'm irritated that she's acting different and I'm unsatisfied with myself about the lifestyle I've provided for her or the lack thereof.

My immaturity was at the root of all the arguments, the age difference really started to show. 1 day I playfully threw a cup of water in her face thinking we would have a water fight, boy was I wrong. She pulled a knife on me but I shut the door in between us and held it until she calmed down. Later I realized that wasn't a good move especially for a woman who had been physically abused. My 21 year old intentions were to have fun but her 30 year old personality saw that as an act of disrespect. Her car broke down a couple days after we arrived in Georgia so I had to jump into 2 car payments for us both so she could look for work while I was at work on base instead of having to pick me up and drop me off every day. This inflated my immature ego even more, never have I ever contributed this much to not only my own life but someone else's and I felt important. I would threaten to take it back when I got angry at something she did or said, I was an emotional child dealing with an emotionally damaged woman.

My mother called me asking for help because once again my aunt had put her and the rest of my immediate family out. My lady and I loaded up her son and drove both our cars up to Baltimore to bring them down to Georgia with us. She was a country girl so the congested traffic of the DMV overwhelmed her and frustrated me. I argued with her on the way up for missing turns, not following close enough or just plain getting lost. I should've been more appreciative that she took that 12 hour drive with me but I was in my own head about things that were so insignificant I can't even remember. When we made it to our destination I made sure they were checked into a hotel and I went to visit my wife, I say wife because my divorce wouldn't be finalized for another couple months. I only wanted my things that I left behind like my original High School Diploma, my all-star football and lacrosse jerseys for making the city teams and my Athlete of the Year plaque I won my senior year of high school. I wanted to frame those to have something to show my children.

When I arrived to her address it looked abandoned, just when I was about to head back to my car she comes walking out of another house a couple homes down; she had intentionally given me the wrong address. I walked up to front yard gate, as she raised her head to see me walking up she threw her hands in the air and ran back in the house. I could see a bunch of people in there and just like my father I realized I was outnumbered so I hopped back into my car and sped off. I guess she thought I was coming to hurt her but I only wanted my stuff.

I had enough time to cool off so vengeance was the last thing on my mind. However I didn't know what she or her family had up their sleeves so I made sure to take my pistol with me the next day. I knocked on her door the following morning, her sister answered with a scared look on her face she told me to hold on and closed the door. The door swung open again with a light skinned, dirty nigga on the other side, he tried to look cool by taking a pull on his cigarette. "Stay cool" I thought to myself as I asked to see my wife, he told me she was sleep so I walked back to my car.

"I should shoot this mafucka up" I thought, nah I thought about all the children that were in there. I drove off feeling like a bitch for not doing anything to the guy but I know it was the smart thing to do. I didn't get far before I got a call from her asking me what I wanted, "My diploma and jerseys" I replied. "What would you do for it? How much would you pay for them?" My blood started to boil, I couldn't believe this bitch was trying to sell me MY things that I worked hard for. "I should turn this mafucka around and air that bitch out" I thought briefly but I kept driving. "I'm not paying for shit I worked for, you can throw it away" I screamed at her angrily and hung up. That experience really made me hate her even more so than the cheating. She knew how much those things meant to me and she hung them over my head and years later I found out she really did throw them away. What a ruthless bitch, I left Baltimore immediately after that experience with my family.

The crazy thing is I didn't know how to turn off my aggression and I brought that into my new relationship with this southern woman whose demeanor was very different from what I was accustomed to. She was soft spoken, didn't like confrontation which is a good thing but I was too immature to recognize it. At that time I saw her as weak, I picked arguments to pull her aggression out. Whenever I got really angry in an argument I would tell her she could get out and go back to Alabama. I didn't mean it of course that's just what I was accustomed to seeing growing up, putting people out was what I thought was a sign of power. One day I came home to an empty apartment, she called my bluff and was gone. That comfort I had of someone being by my side was gone, anger and despair set in and a void in my happiness was created. Make no mistake about it I was happy but I had a dysfunctional way of showing it. To make the situation even worse I found out a month or so later that she was indeed pregnant with a baby girl so I would be a father soon.

That experience with my ex-wife reinforced the dogma taught to me by my family. The irony is I didn't believe it at first, if I had it would've possibly saved me some heartache. Even though I was essentially warned they didn't teach me anything to combat the manipulation they knew would surely come. It definitely changed me and I didn't have the tools to identify or navigate the trauma. Unfortunately this would lead to a long line of hurt women starting with my daughter's mother. We've reconciled since and will always have love for each other but these two experiences where the Genesis of the Crook.

Waste of Money

About 2 weeks into my new employee orientation in Kuwait I was talking to my instructor about the culture shock and he explained proper ways to conduct myself to not break any local laws. He told me how damn near everything had mobile services including manicures, pedicures and massages. "Give me your address I'm going to send my masseuse over today on me as a Welcome to Kuwait." I thought to myself that he was a pretty cool dude to do that for me and I've never had a massage at that point so I was excited. The doorbell to my apartment rings that evening and I open to find 2 little Chinese women smiling at me, they may have been 5ft tall maybe 120lbs each. Which didn't bother me I wasn't trying to fuck they were there to give me a massage. "Why 2?" I thought to myself as I let them in but I figured he had told her how big I was so she brought help, I was 6'5" about 350lbs at that time. I had a roommate because it was company provided housing so I told him I was about to get a massage as we passed his room.

We walk into my room and before I could get my door closed one of the women drops to her knees, pulls my dick out and starts sucking; the other starts getting undressed. "OH SHIT!!!" I thought to myself as the naked one says "40 KD" (Kuwaiti Dinar), What the fuck could I say but "OK" as one women sucks my dick & the other sucks and plays with my nipples. The naked one leaves out the room to go freshen up I assume while I lay on my bed and let the other continue giving me head. As I lay back I'm thinking "Nigga are you really about to pay for a piece of ass?" I replied to myself "Hell Naw I'm about to pay for 2 asses." The other walks back in and closes the door and they swap out as the 1st one gets undressed now. I will say they were a little too clean and proper for my liking. I wanted that porn head with one on my balls and one on my dick at the same time. They wiped my dick down before they sucked as they passed it back and forth which was kind of annoying. I wasn't attracted to them but the excitement of having 2 women at the same time kept me hard.

One stops as the other pulls out a condom, she puts it on and sits on my dick slowly, I'm not small so she didn't sit all the way on at 1st she had to work it in but she took it all eventually. Her boney ass slamming down on my pelvis actually hurt so there was no pleasure in that part, I was just counting down to when she would stop. She did after 5 minutes or so and the other swapped out a fresh condom and cleaned me up before hopping on. She was a little thicker so it didn't hurt, that was a relief. It felt good but not enough for me to cum so after 5 minutes or so they start telling me to cum and the other starts rubbing under my balls and gooch area real aggressive. I abruptly stopped her from doing that bullshit, "I don't know what kind of freaky shit dudes be having these hoes doing" I thought. The excitement was gone now so I jerked off and nutted on their titties. They cleaned me and themselves up and left after I paid them.

I walk to my roommates room to tell him what just happen but he already knew and was cracking up. "She came in and asked me if I wanted to join" he said, that was kind of embarrassing. He told me that was normal around Kuwait though and nothing to be ashamed of. "I recognized her when she came in, she's always around her" he said, "Nigga why didn't you say anything?" I asked. "You're were going to find out real soon" he retorted and I did so he had a point. My instructor was really the muthafuckin man in my opinion after that because that was one hell of an experience. I wouldn't pay for anymore ass after that I thought but of course I would, I'll get to that in a minute. When I came to work the next day my grin told my instructor everything he needed to know. I told him how much I paid and he let me know that I had been hustled. I completely forgot that he told me he paid her already as a gift to me so she got paid twice. It wasn't much money so I found it amusing and we laughed about it.

About a month after that I realized getting some more ass would be quite a task. Most of the women I saw had little or no experience speaking English and the American women had their noses so far in the air I wouldn't dare try to speak. One day as I rode in a taxi back from the grocery store I playfully asked the driver "Where the hoes at?" He was an East Indian guy who spoke English pretty good so he understood what I meant and replied "I have friend who can get whatever you want." He gives me his friends number and It dawned on me that these are more than likely hookers and I would have to pay. I had always thought of paying for pussy as lame but that 3some experience shifted my views on the matter a little. So I call the number and the Madam asks me which race or ethnicity I wanted in particular, I didn't have a clue or care so I told her to choose. I'm honestly nerves as hell thinking "Nigga are you really about to pay for some pussy AGAIN?" I shamefully answered myself "Yes, Yes I am" I had to get some because jerking off was more of a nuisance than satisfaction at this point.

About an hour passed before I got a call saying they were in the lobby of my apartment building and was on the way up. I opened my door to two East Indian women coming out of the elevator and directly into my apartment without saying a word. Straight into my room we go as I introduce myself, they did the same as they smiled nervously because I was probably the biggest person they've ever seen; at least in person. "20 KD and you call me when your done" the madam said to me as I opened my wallet to pay. After paying the Madam she left & we got right to it. It wasn't exciting enough to detail but it was the beginning of a "tricking" spree. At least twice a week I was calling up the Madam, ordering women was as easy as ordering pizza. "Hey let me get a sri lankan this time", "I'll take an Ethiopian this time" and this list goes on. It was almost addictive to have a woman sexually and not have to put in a bunch of time talking my way into her panties.

This would come to an abrupt end when I realized the possibilities of what the women's reality was. One day I place an order for an Indian woman and when they arrived the woman seemed a little more timid then the others. She stood in between my legs as I sat on the edge of the bed and I started to rub her ass as she wrapped her arms around my neck. I pulled her pants and panties down at the same time to get a better feel. As I ran my hands across her ass I felt a scar, then another and another it seemed like her ass was covered with them. I turned her around and it was evident that this woman had definitely been whipped. At that moment my eyes were opened wide to human trafficking and I felt horrible. I thought women were just trying to make extra money it never dawned on me that at least some of these women were forced. I honestly didn't know what to do so I pulled her pants up and asked if she was hungry, she had a confused look on her face and said nothing. I can't remember what I made but I made her a plate anyway.

As she ate laying across my bed I showed her old pictures and told stories behind some of them. She couldn't speak much English but she understood what I was saying. She finished her food, layed down next to me and started to rub on my back. Kisses followed and before my sympathy for her could overpower my lust I was putting on a condom and sliding inside of her. Her vibe had changed from when she 1st came in, she was more relaxed, for the most part she fucked me. It excited me to see her thrusting her pelvis against mine, moaning and taking charge from every position we got into. We ended on our side; as she threw her little light brown skinned ass back on my dark chocolate manhood I noticed the condom broke. "Oh well nigga you done already exchanged fluids" I thought to myself, I didn't miss a stroke before blasting off inside of her without a care in the world. When I tried to move my arm from around her stomache she gripped it and held me tight, even lock her legs behind mine. She wanted to be held apparently and I obliged by staying inside of her, holding her tight and rubbing my beard on the back of her neck. We laid there for a good 20 minutes before I called her ride, she cleaned the both of us up and left.

After that I made the decision to not trick off anymore and in the back of my head I'll always wonder if I have a half Indian child out in the world somewhere. I wondered if she would be beaten if she was pregnant, I thought about calling the madam to ask about her. I also thought about me being Captain Save-A-Hoe but was she really a hoe? I thought; because I didn't think she was doing this of her own free will. Then I thought about if I really wanted any issues in this foreign country with people who were in their element so I let any thoughts of reconnecting with her go. I had to do the work of actually burning my time up trying to talk my way into some pussy or better yet try not to talk my way out of some. I've heard that men can't talk their way into some ass because women know within the 1st few minutes of meeting you if they'd fuck you it's just our job not to fuck it up by saying the wrong thing. Great piece of advice that I'll share how I applied that in a later story. I was able to get with a few women mostly American during my stay in Kuwait but paying for any was not an option.

After coming back from overseas and trying to attend college I decided becoming a truck driver was best for me. I was assigned a trainer named Damon who I had to drive with for a couple months. He would frequent strip clubs and as you could imagine I followed, better than sitting in a truck I guess. The 1st strip club we went to was in New Jersey, I was nervous as hell. I tossed a few dollars and watched women dance but at midnight they would turn things up a notch. The DJ yelled "Who's birthday is it this week?" as 2 guys raised their hands. They went on stage as the female bartender instructed security to lock the front door. She went on stage with another dancer and they proceeded to suck those dude's dick in front of everybody. I WAS FLABBERGASTED!!!!! I could not believe what I saw, my heart was racing with excitement and a bit of disgust. I definitely thought stuff like this didn't happen in real life but I was wrong. What made me cringe even more was when the bartender's boyfriend came to pick her up as the club closed. She kissed him oh so passionately as we stood across the street laughing.

Even though I laughed I felt sorry for the guy because it was obvious he had no clue and she had him wrapped around her finger. A few weeks later we went to another New Jersey strip club and my experience was better than the last. We sat at the bar as a pretty dark-skinned bartender/dancer served us. She introduced herself by her stage name "Shotgun", she asked us questions about ourselves, talked about herself a little; she knew how to carry a conversation for sure. In that conversation we learned that she was in her mid 40's which we couldn't believe. She was the finest woman in the club, body was nice and tight, plump round ass and her skin looked smooth as hell. Once she came from around the bar and gave me a lap dance I learned that her skin was in fact smooth. Not only that she smelled GREAT!!!! She told me she showered periodically throughout her shift in response to my compliments. Honestly the 1st club I went to and the one I was in at this time had a bunch of funky women walking around shaking ass.

Shotgun asked me to turn back towards the bar as I had spun around to get my lap dance from her earlier. She started giving me a neck and back massage right there at the bar. I was in heaven, her hands were soft but she had a firm grip. She whispered in my ear about how a man should be treated and I deserved it. It felt so good drool started running out of my mouth a little, I had to snap out of the trance when the realization came that I was still in the club. When she finished I turned around and stuffed 3 $20 bills into her bra as she kissed me on the cheek. At that point she had my mind and I was basically eating out the palm of her hand. I couldn't see any woman in the club but her after that. I held in a slight jealousy I felt as she made her way around the small club flirting and giving lap dances to other guys. In my short time at this club she gave me more attention and affection I've ever gotten at one time in my life. If any phrase best fits this situation it would be "I'm in love with a stripper".

She invites me to a corner of the club for more lap dances, as she continues to give me compliments and affection. My dick is rock hard at this point and she grabs it to position it in a way that she could grind her pussy directly on it as she gives me a lap dance. I'm definitely ready to fuck now so I pulled my dick out, "O no baby I don't grind on raw dick" She whispered to me as she put it back in my shorts. My feelings were hurt, I do not take rejection well so when she finished I decided to wait for Damon outside. Maybe 10-15 minutes later Shotgun comes out fully dressed and sits next to me on the abandoned steps next door. She gave me more personal information about herself including her real name, she told me she didn't sell her pussy and she knew her grinding on my raw dick would give the wrong impression. "I will suck a dick for $250" she blurted immediately after, it caught me off guard so all I could do was laugh. "Damn I wish I didn't spend all my money on lap dances" I thought, o yea as horny as she had me I would've paid her for it. I told her next time I came through I would definitely take her up on that. That experience was addicting and would lead me from strip club to strip club chasing that feeling.

The next strip club Damon took me to was in Chicago, a hood spot where the chicks barely danced. I had about $60 on me and that was my limit, after I threw that I would be done. Almost immediately after entering the club a dancer walks up to me and asks if I would like a tour, of course I accepted. She was dark-skinned, fairly tall about 5'9" with a nice body, I stared in amazement as she led me around. We get to a more intimate area with a security guard at the door and tells me I had to pay him $5 to enter the area. My curiosity had me all in so I did, inside there were half cubicles like you would find in an office building. As we walk down the aisle she says "As you can see that's how we get down here" nodding to a customer getting a lap dance in a cubicle to our left. As I did a double take I realized dude's pants were around his ankles, the chick was riding him not giving him a lap dance. The adrenaline running through me was something I never felt before, I was excited and nervous. "You want your dick sucked or some pussy?" she asked as I stuttered trying to find my words.

"I only have $60" I mumbled to her while patting myself on the back for not bringing in more money. I knew my willpower was not that strong to have cash on me and not spend it. "There's an ATM by the front door" she replied confidently. "Fuck!!!!" I thought to myself as I took the walk of shame. If you have to use the ATM at a strip club you're probably spending money than you should. I felt like all eyes were on me and to make sure no other chick snatched me up she followed me to the ATM. Rubbing my back as I punched in my pin number I felt super lame but that was not about to stop me from getting my dick wet. She charged $100 for a blowjob and another $60 for pussy so I took out $100 just in case the head was good enough that I wanted to fuck. We went back to the cubicle, she put a condom on me with her mouth and went to work. It was ok, I'm not a fan of condoms so getting my dick sucked with one was really wack.

I look up to the aisle to see the dancer that was just fucking a guy looking at us, licking her tongue at me and squeezing her titties. That completely confused me so I cracked a nervous smile and put my focus back onto the chick I was with. The head started to get boring so I slid the extra $60 out my pocket and gave it to her, she knew what that meant. She bent over the chair I sat in and I began fucking her doggy style. At this point the excitement is gone and she seemed to be enjoying it more than I was so I faked a cramp in my leg and stopped. She massaged my imaginary cramp as I told her I was good, we could stop now. I didn't understand at the time why strip clubs were so addictive to me back then. Now I know I liked the attention and physical affection women gave me in the clubs. Even though they were just after money I was ok with that. The way I see things is time is more valuable than money, I'd rather spend money on a woman I'm not that interested in than my time. Money can be replaced, time can't so as long as I felt good in the moment it was money well spent as far as I was concerned.

I let myself believe the lie in the moment, it was a bit of an escape. At that point in my life even in situationships and relationships women were draining me financially and/or emotionally but they weren't affectionate enough to satisfy my thirst for feminine energy or treating me well enough. I mean if your stressing me the fuck out at least have moments when you make me feel like something special. "Why bother" I thought to myself about getting into an emotional relationships versus tricking off at strip clubs. Wasn't long before I noticed the more clubs I went to the lazier the women got. I noticed the younger women didn't really understand how they could talk their way into more money than shaking their ass or they just didn't know how to talk to men. The clubs started being so dull I would walk in sit down for a few minutes, hand my stack of $1 bills to the closest stripper and walk out. I realized that feeling Shotgun gave me, I wouldn't find again; at least not in a strip club. At that point since I was no stranger to flat out buying pussy I thought "Why not?". At least this way I could skip the politics of a being in a club and have a more direct approach to what I wanted.

I played with the idea shortly but I wasn't about to pick up any hookers off the street so I put that idea away. I'm living in Alabama at this time when I started back on dating sites and it wasn't long before I started talking to a chick that held my attention. Only issue was she lived about 45 minutes away in Tennessee, I was willing to drive to meet her but before I could she told me she coming into town to a local club and would swing by my place. She text me to see if I was still awake around 3a.m., of course I had been because I didn't want to miss her.

She let me know she was headed my way and I waited in anticipation. 3am was definitely booty call hours so I knew fucking was on the table. I get another text saying she's walking up to my door, I opened to find her standing there looking better than her pictures. She may have been 5'5" or so about 200lbs, thick is how I prefer my women. Light-skinned, pretty light brown eyes, thick lips and an even thicker country ass Tennessee accent that turned me on. There wasn't a bit of nervousness present, we joked and talked for a little while before things got physical.

Cuddling turned to kissing which turned to panties coming off & my face smothered in pussy. I LOVE "eating" pussy, the reaction from women gave me motivation and enthusiasm to give my best performance. After she came a couple times I slid into her unprotected and it was lovely. We switched positions a few times since I had always had issues with finishing during sex I finished myself as she played with my nipples to assist. We cuddled again as I feel asleep. I wake up a few hours later and she was gone. I felt violated a little because she didn't wake me, just left like I was some hoe who didn't mean anything. I guess that was karma because I'm sure I've done that to others a few times. I text her later that day and of course her explanation was that she didn't want to wake me up. I pretty much was her after the club dick for a couple months, no dates just late night hook ups and pillow talk. Damn near every time I awoke to her being gone, I got use to it.

All of a sudden we started grabbing a bite to eat from Krystal's in the early morning hours, that became our routine for a while. Then she started actually spending the night and without an official conversation things blossomed into a relationship. We started going places together, I even let her meet my daughter. I woke up to message one day from her Facebook profile asking me how I'm doing which was weird since we always communicated through text or phone calls. Turns out it was her ex-boyfriend, he started running down my life story to me. I was full of rage, everything I've told her she told to him. I cursed him out then called her to do the same. She was completely blindsided and told me they were still friends that's why she told him about me. "I don't know why he hacked my page or hit you up, he's never done that with none of the other guys I've dated" She said as I calmed myself down. Her response made sense so I told her if that shit happened again I'd be done with her, I did not like drama. I quickly swept that under the rug and kept on the course we were on.

I would drive up to Tennessee to see her sometimes since she took the initiative most times to drive down to see me. I liked how quiet she was, we made jokes and talked but she didn't just run her mouth unnecessarily. On the other hand she wasn't nurturing at all by my standards, she didn't cook for me or cater to me when I was a guest in her home at all. There was a nonchalant attitude that irritated and intrigued me. One night I was over her house and we were getting it in as usual, I remember looking at her clock as my face sunk between her thighs; 4 a.m. it read. About halfway through my feast I feel like someone is watching me but I shook that thought off telling myself I was trippin. I didn't stop to look because I was on a mission. We finished up and I asked her to bring me a glass of water which she rarely did but she agreed. As I lay naked in her bed with a big grin on my face feeling accomplished I hear her front door slam shut. I jump up walk into her living room which was a short distance because she had a one bedroom apartment, I hear a bang on the door.

Once I realize she wasn't in the apartment anymore I swing the front door open to find her still naked holding some dude from coming into the apartment. I run to throw on my pants and came back to address him, by that time he started retreating back to his car. I think once he saw how big I was he didn't want that problem, I was 6'5" about 450lbs at the time. I ran down the apartment steps and caught him before he got to his car. "Naw man she lying" he blurted out as he pulled his phone out suggesting he had something to show me. I snatched his phone to find a text message thread between the 2 of them. I start scrolling through as she walks up to us after getting dressed. "I'm cooking tonight, you want some?" one message from her read, among others of her offering quality time she had yet to offer me. "I just came to give her house key back" He said as he hands her a key, I hand him his phone and tell him to get the fuck on. We argue after he leaves, turns out that was the same ex-boyfriend that messaged me on Facebook. She gives me a bullshit story about how he had a key to check on her dog while she's gone. I left and told her to never contact me again.

About a week goes by before I get a text from her asking if she could come talk to me. I agreed mainly because I was bored and I was a little interested in what she had to say. We sit in my room as she continues apologizing and giving me the same lame story and I got irritated after a while. I did miss her and

I wanted to believe her but my ex-wife's infidelity had made this kind of situation all the more touchy. Finally I had enough and I told her to leave, she refused and begged me to take her back. I grabbed her arm and started pulling her out of my room when she dropped to her knees. I grabbed at her again while opening my door and began pulling her to my front door. Halfway through my living room I looked down and noticed I was pulling her by her hair. I let her go and she immediately crawled back into my room. I've watched my mother and other women be beaten up and I didn't want to be that type of man.

I made my mind up that I wouldn't try to make her leave physically. I walked back to my room and sat on my bed as she continued to plead with me. I looked away hoping she would realize there was no getting through to me and leave. Instead she started unbuckling my belt, "Fuck" I thought because I knew I didn't have enough discipline to stop her. She drops to her knees and starts giving me head, I just laid back and let it happen. That turned to full blown make up sex and just like that we were back together. Not because the sex was just that great but after the sex when I was emotionally vulnerable the pillow talk got to me. Didn't take long for us to get back into our routine of late night booty calls. Maybe a month or so went by and yet again another incident. I was up at her place laying across the bed when her phone went off next to me, she was in the kitchen cooking.

I looked at the message as I brought her the phone, I can't remember what the message said but something was off. The contact read "Aunt Pat" but the message definitely didn't seem like it came from a woman or relative. I read it aloud, her eyes bucked as she came rushing to me to retrieve her phone. I turned my back and started scrolling through the message thread and I realize it's the same nigga, she disguised his number as a relative. I threw her phone in the toilet as she was tugging on me the whole time trying to get it back. Turns out it was waterproof so no damage but she starts going off yelling at me which really triggered me. I saw red for a moment and grabbed both her arms and shook her a few times.

My rage subsided enough for my rational mind to kick in, "GET THE FUCK OUT OF HERE" I thought as I made my way to the door and left. I was legitimately hurt from those experiences. Overall I felt stupid for not leaving her alone from the 1st incident, then there was me having to explain to my daughter why she wouldn't be around anymore. Then there was the shame of me being pulled out of character in a way that made me feel disgusted. After that I told myself I would never be with a woman that would get me that mad. It seemed like the drama excited her but she had no idea how crazy I could get when pushed and for both our sakes I wouldn't stick around to find out. After that I decided no more relationships for me for a while, I took a break from dating in general.

Eventually I found out about escort sites and I would browse through the profiles, window shopping if you will. I talked myself out of actually calling any of them for a few months. At this point in my life I wasn't looking for affection or attention, I just wanted to bust a nut without using my own hand. One day my hormones had built up enough for me to make the call to an ad. She advertised $50 for a QV (Quick Visit-15mins), $80 for 30 minutes and $120 for an hour. Well to be accurate she used words like "roses" and "donation". I guess hookers thought that was some clever code that would throw cops off. I drove trucks over the road at this time so I waited in my truck for her arrival. I was nervous as hell, thinking of every possible scenario including cops showing up to my truck instead of the woman in the pictures. I even thought about parking in a different location and turning my phone off but my raging hormones broke through my fear and told me to stay the course.

She called me when she arrived as she walked up to my truck, I let her in as I looked her over to make sure she was as thick as she looked in her photos. I sat on the bed in the sleeper portion of my truck and handed her the money. "Uh Uh" she replied to my gesture, "Never hand a woman money, sit it down in plain sight" she said as she schooled me on the protocol of buying pussy. I took my shorts off and laid back as she unwrapped a condom and put in on me with her mouth. I was amazed at how she was able to do it so effortlessly until I remembered this was a professional. I couldn't get past not being able to feel anything but the pressure her lips applied. I kept going limp because my mind was all over the place. I gathered my focus enough to get my little guy back up so I could fuck her doggystyle.

She was dripping wet, I felt it as I used my hand to guide myself into her. Again with the lack of sensation from the condom, I felt the warmth and the pressure her pussy applied to me but I couldn't feel her juices; I heard them though. When I started to get bored I figured I'd rap things up. I asked her to suck and play with my nipples while I masturbate. Yea I'm a nipple guy and I'm not ashamed. I got off in a minute or so and she cleaned me up with some baby wipes I had on my truck. This was one of a few experiences that went pretty well but there were a lot more bad ones. Some women loved to fuck and this was a way of them not feeling so used by men. Some just needed the money and chose selling ass as a method to get it. I didn't like those type because they usually had bad attitudes and/or no enthusiasm. That would be a complete turn off and I would almost immediately regret it.

One time in particular I hit a chick up on another online ad, this time I was home in my apartment and we agreed that she would come to me. She shows up and as we make our way to my room she's giving me a laundry list of what she doesn't do. "No kissing, No Hugging, No positions other than doggy style" she listed off among other things. " You're a hoe, hoes aren't supposed to come with rules" I thought as I second guessed did I even want to attempt this bullshit. She smelled like cigarettes which absolutely disgusted me. If I reject her services without paying she could cause a scene I thought. "I don't suck dick" cut through my internal thoughts as I looked at her like she was out of her fucking mind. "You don't suck dick?" I replied to get confirmation which she confirmed. "I'm cool on that, you can keep the money."

"You don't want nothing?" She replied as I pointed to the money I laid out on my dresser. I shook my head basically declining, "I can come back when I'm off the clock, I suck dick when I'm off the clock". "This bitch is fucking nuts", I thought to myself as I declined again as I walked her out. She obviously wasn't doing this full time, no way she was making any money with all those rules. When these kinds of experiences started becoming the majority I slowed up and ultimately stop tricking. The physical affection and attention I got in strip clubs was no where to be found when dealing with "escorts" and the sex more than likely was mediocre at best. There really wasn't any fulfillment coming from those transaction. Instead of money well spent it turned out to be a Waste of Money.

Feel It All

"In the night, I hear 'em talk the coldest story ever told; somewhere far along this road, he lost his soul to a woman so heartless." Blasts out the speakers of my 2006 Grand Marquis early one morning as I head into base for Physical Training. Kanye West really hit the nail on the head with this one I thought as tears roll down my face. That song was the soundtrack to my life at that point. I felt numb to life, just going through the motions of working daily and the drive in between. The only thing that made me feel better was sex, well the affection that came with it. Dating sites were really starting to gain momentum and I was on a few. A little conversation, a date or an invite over to my place and I would be deep in some pussy not too long after. I never really understood how, I didn't talk much and I definitely didn't feel like I looked good enough. I thought they were just into me because I was in the military.

I tried to talk to a fellow military woman online but she told me her sister saw my profile and was interested. I was a little disappointed but I figure her sister couldn't look too much different so I got a couple pics, all headshots of course. She wasn't as fine as her sister but I could work with her, we made plans to chill together and I actually picked her up. We hit it off pretty good, riding back to my place we're just laughing and having a good time. In the midst of her telling me a joke I look over to notice she doesn't have a hand. Well she had a hand but it was deformed, it reminded me of a T-Rex arm. I was shocked but hopefully I didn't show it but my plan remained the same I was going to fuck her regardless. I remember stroking her from behind and wondering how she was keeping her balance with only one working hand. I chuckled to myself as I fucked her silly and all the noises she made kept me excited enough to stay up despite thinking about all the jokes in this situation. I don't think she got much attention because she was very appreciative of the little time I spent with her, even giving me head on the way back to drop her off.

When God close one door he opens another I thought because I basically got rejected by her sister but got her, she was a freak too. I knew I would never see or talk to her again but I made all kinds of promises leaving her with a little hope. My mind was on the next piece of pussy I would surely get. Karma is a motherfucker though because the next chick I got with taught me a lesson. Her profile on line screamed slut, she had her titties out, lingerie on etc. Middle aged chick who honestly looked below average but she had sex appeal and I wanted to smash. She lived about 20 minutes from me so we made plans to get together.

She was waiting for me with lingerie on and candles lit when I arrived to her place, she was ready and so was I. She told me her bed was broken so we had to fuck on an air mattress in the living room. I guess some other dude put in work and broke it but that didn't stop me from wanting to get my piece. I even went in her raw, I didn't realize it then but I didn't value myself or care if I lived or died. We fucked and sucked for an hour or so and I went home. I planned on seeing her again because the sex was good and that was hard to come by. The sex I usually had was with women who didn't really embrace themselves sexually but not this slut. She knew exactly what she wanted and how to get it.

Three days later I notice a wet spot in my boxer briefs which I initially ignored thinking it may have been pre-cum from one of my many dirty thoughts. Then I went to take a piss and it burned a little. I still wasn't sure so I waited a day to notice a brownish discharge coming out of my dick. "I know this bitch didn't burn me" I thought. Like Déjà vu in a way I went to my father and told him I may have been burned. He immediately told me to show my mother and not him which I did. "Yup you burning" she said at first glance and I was embarrassed to say the least. "I'm going to kill this bitch" I thought, unlike when I thought the same thing about Rochelle this time I had the means to do so. I bought a little .380 handgun a couple months after I moved to Georgia. First I had to get treated though so off to hospital I went where the doctor put a small Q-tip inside my dick to take a sample for testing. A shot and prescription for antibiotics cleared everything right up.

That night I took my pistol and headed out to ole girl's house. She lived in a housing project so I parked across the street at a closed gas station and walked over. It was about 1 a.m. so nobody was outside, I knocked a few times as I held my gun against my thigh. I knocked a few more times and called her a couple times, she text me back saying she was out of town. Riding back home I thought to myself how lucky she was, the reality was I was the lucky one. I would've ruined my life one way or the other, even if I would've gotten away with it my conscience would have sent me to an early grave. I realized I shouldn't blame her, it was my decision to screw her unprotected and the STD was a consequence I had coming. So once I came to that realization harming her in any way was out of my head completely, I just would never mess around with her again. You would think getting burned would slow me down and it may have a little but it didn't stay that way.

I was back on those dating sites and back to screwing random women regularly. It wasn't necessarily intentional though, I would meet a chick we would hit it off, have sex and my interest would fade or we would argue about something insignificant. The actual sex was the least satisfying part of these encounters. The physical affection of having my back, head or ears rubbed is what made me feel cared for. Naturally when two people rub and kiss on each other sex comes. I noticed after foreplay most women didn't rub or kiss me once the main event got going and therefore my interest would fade away during sex. Sometimes I would think "look at this lazy bitch" she got me all worked up to just lay back and want me to do everything, sometimes I would be so turned off I would even go limp. I would go from feeling nurtured to abandoned within the matter of minutes.

I remember being so horny one day I fucked 4 women in the same day. Literally breakfast, lunch, dinner and late night snack, I had all of them make me a meal. I washed up in between all but the last one because it was unexpected. When she went down on me I wondered if she could smell the last woman's juices still on me, she didn't stop so I guess not. I was a dirty dick back then who almost never used protection. The most precaution I took was when I got a refill on antibiotics I would take a couple anytime I fucked a chick I thought might have had something. "If she is burning these will knock it out" I would say to myself and go on about my day. On occasion I would get a good 5 or 6 women who were pretty cool and I got into situationships with them. We weren't officially in relationships but we acted like it and all of them thought they were my only woman. I would tell them I loved them and anything else that would keep them focused on me. I didn't want them dealing with any other guys so I attached myself to them emotionally.

The problem with that is they all had different personalities and needs, I was worn out emotionally and mentally trying to keep up with all of them. I didn't want to dump anybody because I would feel like an asshole so I would become an asshole to make them break up with me, weird how that made sense at the time. I felt better knowing that they chose to end things rather than having them possibly feeling like they lacked something. Some didn't seem to want relationships just sex which I had mixed feelings about. On one hand I felt relieved that I didn't have to figure out how to get rid of them on the other I felt like I wasn't in control. Those women challenged me in a way that I've yet to fully understand.

One in particular was from the same town in Georgia as the chick who burned me. She would come into my town to club every now and then and she would stop by my place to get broke off before she went back home. We fucked at my place, in my car, out in the woods, pretty much any and everywhere with very little conversation. I only knew her 1st name which didn't occur to me until I needed to know her full name, I'll get to that in a second. After a few months of fucking around she stopped coming by and stopped communication all together. I didn't think much of it because I had plenty of other options. One Saturday morning around 4 a.m. about 4 months later I'm woken up to someone knocking on my door. As I swung my front door open there she stood holding what appeared to be a .38 revolver staring directly into my eyes. My heart pounding with fear as she said "You better not have a bitch in here".

All I could do was crack a nervous smile as she pushed passed me making her way to my room, luckily I was alone that night. Once she sees that I'm alone she puts her gun away and orders me to fuck her. At this point I'm turned on like a muthafucka, "This bitch is crazy" I thought as my manhood rose for the occasion. She flips her sundress up and leans across my bed and I started giving her some pretty solid backshots. I reach around to grab her titties but my hand brushes against her stomach 1st and it's hard. Then it hits me, SHE'S PREGNANT. I didn't stop fucking though but afterwards I asked her why she never told me anything. She told me it might not be mine and I didn't have to worry she could raise the child by herself, there was no way I was about to let a child of mine grow up without me. We cuddled and went to sleep, when I woke up later that morning she was gone.

That's when I realized I didn't know her last name, where she lived exactly or anything that could help me find her. She stopped answering my calls that day and removed her profile on the dating website that I met her on. Luckily about 6 months later I was talking to a female from the town and she recognized her from my description and told me where she lived. One weekend when I got off of work I drove out to her house, at this point she should've given birth by now. I knocked on the door with butterflies in my stomach expecting her to open the door holding an infant with my big ears. The door cracked open as 2 of her children stuck their heads out, I asked to speak with their mother and they closed the door. Then I hear some commotion inside so I press my ear to the door. "Go out the back and creep up on him from the side" says a male voice and others confirming the plan.

I peek around the side of the house to see dudes coming out the back door. RUN!!! I thought but my ego wouldn't let me take off running but I did briskly walk back to my car. I was driving away by the time they got to the front of the house, there were about 6 of them. I guess she was in a relationship, not sure for how long; maybe that's his baby I thought as I made my way home. Either way I probably would never find out because I wasn't coming back to drama and I doubted she would reach out to me. I told myself the child wasn't mine and I moved on.

Almost every night I would lay in bed thinking about those miserable days back home with Rochelle and the drama that ensued during basic training. I was going through life numb, going to work everyday then home to loneliness. The only time I felt anything was when I had sex and like I mentioned before the foreplay was the most satisfying. I felt like a failure because my marriage didn't work and that the women giving themselves to me now only did so because I was a soldier. After lashing out at work a few times I was sent to a psychiatrist who diagnosed me with depression and prescribed me some medication for it, I didn't take it for a while though. "I'm not crazy I thought" as I continued living my life wild; having unprotected sex with strangers, making empty promises and just flat out lying. One day in particular I felt really sad so I decided to take the medication I was prescribed. As I sat around waiting for it to kick in I started feeling worse.

"Come back to me" I heard Rochelle's voice whisper to me and the anger from that whole situation came rushing back into my psyche. Then I started thinking about my daughter and how I'm not with her mother, I failed as a father. Why was I even alive? I'm not contributing anything to anybody. I'm better off dead I thought and before I knew it I was staring into my bathroom mirror. Watching tears roll down my face. I must've stood there for at least 15 minutes contemplating how I could end this suffering; end my life. I didn't have any guns so blowing my brains out wasn't an option, stepping out in traffic wouldn't work because there wasn't much in the slow country town I lived in. I had been diagnosed with high blood pressure for which I was on medication so I thought if I took the entire bottle my blood pressure would drop enough to kill me.

Covered in tears & still crying I opened the bottle, tilted my head back and started dumping the pills into my mouth swallowing as many as I could. Then my mood shifted and I thought "I don't want to die", I called an army buddy of mine and told him what I did before hanging up to lay on the floor; I started getting drowsy. He apparently called 911 because I could remember paramedics bursting in my room. Next thing I know I'm in an emergency room drinking "charcoal" as the called it to protect my stomach from the medication I guess. The male nurse shook his head at me like I was a dumb ass and told me I wouldn't have died from taking those medications. I laid there embarrassed waiting to find out when I could be discharged, I was better mentally or so I thought. To my surprised I was informed that I would have to be checked into the psychiatric ward of the hospital for evaluation. "FUCK!!!" I thought; my dumb ass stamped a ticket to the loony bin and there was no way to get out of it. The lights were so bright as a hospital transporter pushed me in a wheel chair up to the psych ward; it felt like the beginning of a scary movie.

As the doors opened to the ward it looked like a stereotypical psych ward in a movie too; people just walking around aimlessly some talking to themselves. One little guy walked up to me and introduced himself, "I'm Raymond Ray Campbell Jr.; I'm also Jesus Christ. Write your name down in my book and today's date." "O shit this dude is really crazy" I thought as I took his composition notebook to do as he asked; no harm to jot down my name no problem. A nurse walked up to me as I finished signing and introduced herself and explained Raymond's deal. He had went through a couple weeks of marine bootcamp and snapped, he thought he was Jesus and wanted everyone who met him to write their names down. There were 2 people per room and doors didn't lock for obvious reasons, I noticed before bed that Raymond was sleeping on the floor. I asked a nurse if she wanted me to help move him, "No we just let him do his thing and sleep where he wants." She just put a pillow under his head and covered him in a blanket. "If I wake up and he's standing over me I'm going to fuck Raymond up", I told the nurse as I walked back to my room.

I got the best sleep I ever had in that place, it was so peaceful and I actually enjoyed talking to the other patients even Raymond. We had group sessions about how to deal with our anxiety and depression, it felt good to talk about my issues without feeling weak. I talked to my daughter's mother on the phone after a couple days and she told me how much my daughter needed me. Even though I wasn't around at the moment it was only temporary, I apologized about the things I felt I did wrong. I asked if we could try to be together again, she told me if I got out I could come back to Alabama and we could give things another shot. That gave me something to look forward to because I was informed I would be given an honorable discharge due to my issues so I know for a fact I was getting out. I was discharged from the hospital after about a week, I didn't know how long it would take for my Army discharge. I kept to myself while I mentally prepared to get out.

A few months later I got the final word that I would be getting discharged soon and I was filled with joy. I hadn't talked to my daughter's mother much because I was getting myself together. I called to tell her I would be coming to her soon and to my surprise she told me she had gotten into a relationship already. That really turned my smile upside down, I was infuriated. I cursed her out and hung up. After that I went back to my comfort activity; FUCKING!!!!! Night after night almost I was in somebody's bed not always a different chick some nights it would be the same one. At one point I allegedly had 5 additional children on the way. I say allegedly because none were ever proven. They all claimed they had an abortion or miscarriages, which worked out in my favor for sure because I would have been screwed with that many children in that stage of my life.

One day I got into my car to head to work to find that my battery was dead, I just replaced it the day prior so now I knew it was my alternator. As I waited for a ride to work an old lady who lived a few trailers down from me came creeping by in her; a Ford Crown Victoria. She was cool, our cars were pretty much the same so we raced a few times for fun. She stopped and told me that her daughter thought I was cute and we should get to know each other. Up until that point I had never met any of her children, Her daughter leaned forward and we said hello to each other. Her mother told us to exchange numbers and before I could get up to walk over the passenger door swung open and she got out. Walking over to me all I could focus on were her big dreamy eyes, dark chocolate brown skin and beautiful smile, 'I'm Lolita" she said; I introduced myself as well. We exchanged numbers and as she walked back to the car I noticed the thick thighs, phat booty and I'm sure she put a little extra swing in her hips because she knew I was watching.

The 1st text I got from her were a few pictures and I couldn't believe it, I saw her online and messaged her a few times over the course of a year or so. I recognized the tattoo of candy on her ass cheek. I felt like I had hit a jackpot, the woman I'd been lusting over had been feeling the same about me. She told me she had 5 children and I immediately thought "Do I give off step daddy vibes?" Another woman with 5 children came strolling into my life which didn't turn me off but I had a feeling she would be emotionally damaged in some way. She told me her friends were coming into town to party that very same night but she wanted to chill with me. Of course I agreed so she had her friends drop her off at my place that night. She called me to tell me she was outside, as I opened the door to meet her I see her 2 friends sitting in the car. It felt like I swallowed my tongue, I had fucked both of her friends; one was the chick who burned me.

I knew this night would not end how I wanted it to because I definitely had to tell her before they did. They didn't say anything when they dropped her off, just a "What's up" nod and off to the club they went. Lolita and I went inside to watch a movie, my priorities weren't in the right place so I didn't have any furniture. She didn't seem to mind as we lay on some blankets I had on the floor and watched a movie on my computer. Once we started rubbing on each other a little I worked up enough courage to tell her. At least I got to feel her up I thought, she didn't seem to mind she just asked how long ago and if I still wanted to mess with them. I definitely didn't so we continue our night with plenty of sex and pillow talk, I took her home the next morning. She came to visit me a few more times and then I started spending time at her place. This was the 1st time since my daughter's mother that I didn't think of being with other women while dealing with someone. I enjoyed spending time with Lolita and her children. I had a family again I thought so that void was filled, temporarily at least.

I had recently been discharged from the army so I had a little money and plenty of free time so we would go shopping and enjoy each other's company. I pretty much lived at her place but I wouldn't dare let my place go. I had seen too many dudes growing up being kicked out of their homes because it wasn't theirs. I would never let a woman be in position to make me homeless again. After a couple months the sex slowed up and the crazy started to really show. She didn't like me wearing basketball shorts or sweatpants outside because my dick print showed. I thought it was cute and funny until one day she threatened to break my car windows if I left the house in shorts. She grabbed a bat and I thought she was really serious so I called the police thinking I would be covering my ass if things got physical. The cops showed up and told me I could be arrested because I wasn't on her lease. I got the fuck out of there and luckily I still had a place to go back to.

Didn't matter much because within 2 days we made up and I was back over there. Once again I'm repeating the same toxic cycle and I thought the drama meant she loved me. One day I couldn't tell you what our argument was about but she insisted on getting out of my car 10 miles away from her place. "To hell with her" I thought as I sped off, continuing to her place to get my things. By the time I arrived she had already called ahead to her sister and told her not to let me in. I didn't cause a scene I just drove home thinking how once again a woman was holding my things over my head. Again "I should shoot that bitches house up" crosses my mind just like I thought with Rochelle. This time however I didn't particularly care if her kids were hurt, I had never been that angry before and it scared me.

I called a friend I met while clearing the base to be discharged and told her what I was feeling. She connected me with the psychiatric ward in the Army hospital and they told me to come check in. A nurse talked to me the entire drive there and even met me in the parking lot. I calmed down within an hour or so and let the staff know that I was alright. As you could imagine getting out wouldn't be so easy and I had to wait a few days to be evaluated again before I was released. Still practicing the same toxic behavior I went back Lolita. I told her what I was thinking and even though she stayed with me things weren't the same and our relationship didn't last much longer. In my childish humor knowing that she was on edge around me I pulled down a dirt road one day deep in the country. She starts getting really nervous asking me where we were going, I didn't say a word.

As I stopped the car I remembered the pocketknife I had in my door so I pulled it out and just stared at her. I looked into those big, dreamy eyes as they filled with tears; it amused me how this mouthy, aggressive woman was so quiet and docile. I burst into laughter as I told her it was all a joke and obviously she didn't find it funny at all. She demanded I take her home and on the way I asked her what was going through her mind. "I wasn't going to see my kids again", at that moment I realized I took things too far. I apologized over and over again during the ride to her place but she wasn't having it at all. After that we pretty much faded away from each other, I don't remember an actual break up conversation.

After that I decided I needed a fresh start so I moved almost 2 hours away. It wouldn't be long before I was out of money, I hadn't found a job and I used my tax money to relocate. It wasn't much because I didn't have a dependent. My daughter's mother claimed her after she told me I could use her on my tax return. She said she would send me $1000 though because I had definitely been as active in my daughter's life as I could've been. I told her she could keep half of what she was going to send me for my daughter. I was confident I would be able to find a job or a way to make some money soon and since I was struggling and couldn't send anything for a month or so I thought it was fair.

Taking advice from an Army buddy I applied for a contracting job in Kuwait, it was a shot in the dark because I didn't meet the qualifications on the job description by a long shot. To my surprise I got a phone interview and job offer, I accepted of course. Only 1 issue though, I needed a passport; not just a passport but an expedited one which cost double. I sold my television and the aftermarket rims on my car to get my passport and other things I needed for the job. A couple weeks pass and I'm literally broke, I made sure my bills were paid but I had no food and my gas tank was on "E". I didn't think much of it because I was still expecting the $500 from my daughter's mother. I called to check on the status of her tax return and I didn't recognize the woman on the phone.

"Yea I got it but I got bills to pay" she said to me more aggressive than I was use to hearing her. "So your not going to send me what you promised?" I asked. "I'm raising my kids by myself, ain't nobody helping me. I need all my money" she blurted out before hanging up on me. I was in shock for a few hours, wondering if she was just angry about something else. I called back thinking she might've calmed down but my phone calls went unanswered. Déjà vu, no longer a child I'm a grown man this time calling on a woman to feed me essentially only this time there was no friendly neighbor I could borrow food from. "How could she turn her back on me" I thought to myself while rubbing her name I had tattooed onto my chest. I'm the same guy who almost went Absent Without Leave (AWOL) to catch my daughter's birth. The same guy who found a way to get our baby a car seat & formula in spite of not being paid in a month due to an Article 15. For those that don't know an Article 15 is basically a punishment in the military where they can take money and/or rank among other things. Hell I just had my daughter in Georgia with me for Christmas and bought her a bunch of stuff.

All I had done up to that point didn't mean anything to her I guess. I didn't understand where this was coming from at all but she was my only hope. I didn't have any friends and my family was struggling themselves, I knew my mother would feed me but I had to get gas money to get there. I didn't call her back the 1st day I just drank tap water and went down memory lane; the good, the bad and the ugly. I had maybe a week left before my trip to Kuwait so I just had to make it until then I thought. Day 2 comes around and I decided to text her asking for $40 which was for gas money to drive to my mother's house. More rejection so tap water and memories for day 2 and my sadness turned to anger. The only thing keeping me sane was knowing I would be leaving soon.

Day 3 comes and I'm definitely starving at this point so I'm begging her for the gas money and around the early afternoon she finally sent it through western union. I drove to the closest western union hoping I didn't run out of gas before I got there. "I can't believe this bitch made me beg for $40 after all I've done" I thought to myself as I made my way to the gas station after picking up the money. I got to my mother's house and ate till I couldn't eat anymore. She gave me some food to take home as well so things worked out. I left for my new job overseas shortly after and put the stress from that situation in my rearview. Even though I had animosity towards my daughter's mother I still offered to send her double the child support she was asking for. With all I had been through in my life the way she treated me wasn't so bad, I just knew when it came down to it she would operate in her own best interest regardless of any agreements or promises she made. I'm the opposite, If I tell someone I'm going to do something I will even at the price of inconveniencing myself.

That experience started bringing me back to reality, like I said before I was walking around numb to life. Even with the pseudo-emotional attachments I made during this period I didn't genuinely feel much. Subconsciously bashing my head up against a proverbial wall which in this case was women. Unprotected sex, multiple partners, an STD, arguments, tears of women I hurt didn't really move me like the betrayal of a woman that gave me my 1st child and I had genuine love for. I believe it was karma but it didn't matter much then it still hurt like hell. Leaving the country helped save me from my self-destructive path. It allowed me to be out of my usual environment that was riddled with so many triggers and I could think about all I had done and try to figure out why. Also most of the women in Kuwait were not my type, I love full figured black women. I was surrounded by boney middle eastern and Asian women so it wasn't too hard to fast from sex. Of course those days were numbered just know I was no longer numb and I could feel it all.

Tender D!#K

Even though I grew up seeing women in charge I also witnessed some abuse. My mother held her own for the most part but other women I knew didn't fair so well. Drug addicted women and some men were routinely disrespected and abused by the local dope boys or their significant others. My environment was so toxic most people would laugh or ignore the assaults all together. I on the other hand would get a gut wrenching feeling of fear, anger and helplessness. One experience I'll never forget took place that summer my parents separated, my big brother stopped by for a visit with his girlfriend. He'd been running the streets since I could remember so I barely saw him and when I did it usually ended in him being violent to someone; this occasion was no different.

I don't know what the argument or disagreement was about but one day as I walked through my aunt's house from the backyard to the front door I could hear his girlfriend crying and pleading for him to stop. As I peaked my head into the narrow hallway leading to the front door I could see him stomping her with so much hatred, disgust & aggression in his eyes. As usual nobody helped; my cousins & I just watched in fear, my aunt did tell him to get out as she made her way downstairs to get to the bottom of the commotion. This solidified the fear I had of him but it hurt and confused me to see his girlfriend get up, fix her clothes and leave with him. Of course I told myself I would never do such a thing to a woman. "What could've set him off?" I thought as I walked out the front door behind them. There was an awkward silence, I could feel the embarrassment on the both of them. My brother always had a short fuse so I just reminded myself of that and tried not to think about it anymore.

Fast-Forward about 9 years to my contracting days; sitting in a pickup truck on a hot Kuwaiti Day in the middle of a dessert in an Ammo Holding Area watching my subordinates load ammunition onto the bed of our truck. I admired them, 120-degree heat & these Indian guys were working their asses off while I had the A/C on full blast. In the distance I see a trail of dust coming from the wheels of a Toyota Camry, "O shit" I thought as I realize my supervisor was coming so I hopped out the truck to act like I was doing some work with the rest of the guys. She pulls up with another woman in the passenger seat, "Hey this is Patrice, she's a supervisor in another section. I said what's up as I looked her over nothing special I thought. No body really, kinda slim which really wasn't my type because I love fat girls & she had buck teeth. I wasn't sexually attracted to her at all, I guess I hadn't been in Kuwait long enough to be that desperate. Shortly after I met her husband at a company meeting, it was definitely a surprise that she had a husband working with the same company. He seemed cool, he was a big guy like myself 6'2" maybe around 300lbs. He was older than me so he would always give me unsolicited lectures and advice.

Now I know he was just doing what men should do by passing wisdom down but back then I resented him for it. So most of his words went in one ear & right out the other. Months went by and I would keep my interactions with him and his wife to a minimum. Hell I wasn't around them much anyway but as my limited sex life continued; my lust for her rose. Her teeth didn't seem so bad all of a sudden, neither did her small frame. I started staring at her a little longer than usual whenever I would be around her. Then light flirting, I never thought there was any chance of me actually fucking her.

Somehow one day I got her yahoo messenger and casually sent her a message. Nothing flirtatious more of a general "Hey how are you" message and we began to chat frequently. I told her about my life back home and she told me about hers. Then she started telling my how she and her husband dabbled in the "Lifestyle". "We've had a threesomes with women and he's fine with that but things changed when we had a foursome." She said before continuing saying that he had gotten jealous of how much pleasure the other guy was giving her. After that things were downhill, apparently he was an abusive guy which was triggering considering my memories of seeing women abused. Learning that really pissed me off and I began to tell her she should leave him. I mean she didn't need him for his money; she was making plenty of her own.

After that conversation I became more hostile towards her husband and more aggressive with my flirtatious energy toward his wife. To the point other co-workers would ask me if we were fucking or did I plan on it. I knew if he pissed her off enough she would fall right into my lap. So I gave her an open invitation to cook dinner for her whenever she had time. She took me up on that offer maybe 2 or 3 weeks later, it was a few days before she went back to the U.S. for some home time. I was excited, can't remember what I cooked but it didn't matter she wasn't interested in food. "I already ate" she replied when I asked if she was ready to eat. "Where's your room?" she asked, I immediately pointed as she made her way deeper into my apartment.

She stripped down to her underclothes & got into bed, I followed her into bed but I got completely naked. Which was shocking because I was nervous as hell. We started kissing, rubbing, you know all the typical foreplay. She licked & played with my nipples which got me standing at attention quickly. Almost just as quickly did she have her lips wrapped around my dick. She had a little mouth so she couldn't help but scrape me with her teeth but I took it so I wouldn't ruin the rhythm we were in. I pulled her up and laid her down so I could return the favor. I kissed her from her neck down to her waistline as she raised her hips to help me get her panties off.

As her panties came off around her feet I kissed from her ankle up to her inner thigh. After a brief pause of nervousness I gave her a soft kiss right on the pussy MUAH!!!!! I was thrown of a bit because I didn't feel any lips, just a soft smooth surface. I gave another kiss with a little tongue at the end to feel around a little bit and still I couldn't feel her lips. The only light in the room is what made its way in from the street lights outside through my window. "Fuck this kissing shit" I thought as I stuck my tongue out to give her one big lick from top to bottom. Still no lips it just felt like a bunch of soft loose skin. I tried not to panic so I said "Fuck It" and used my hand to feel around. Upon my investigation I realized all that loose skin was her pussy lips. I had never seen a pussy that worn out, at least on the exterior.

I had a hard time finding her clit but when I got there that's where I stayed until she came. I fucked her for a few minutes after that; raw of course before finishing myself off. I really like her but the sex was a big disappointment. She stayed for an hour or so afterwards before heading home. We had casual conversation through yahoo messenger while she was on her home time. Maybe a week into her 2 week home time she stopped responded to me and I got worried that something may have happened. My worries were relieved a bit when I saw here driving around at work a couple weeks later but she still wasn't answering my calls or text. I know the sex was trash but to ignore me was completely out of left field. Especially since she had mentioned possibly leaving her husband to be with me.

One day I get a message on yahoo messenger from her telling me that he read her messages and knows that we had sex. In that moment I could only hear my heart pounding against my chest. Before I could respond she told me that she couldn't talk to me anymore and deleted her account. I still can't explain why I was so broken up about it. Maybe it was my fear of rejection or maybe abandonment issues, I couldn't tell you. What I can tell you is I went to work in a daze after that. I told an American co-worker what happened and he told me he heard from a mutual friend that her husband beat her ass because of the affair. That infuriated me and I started going off telling my co-worker/homeboy what I was going to do to him.

"Naw you ain't gonna do all that, she's where she wants to be." Those words were sharp and cut through my rant and brought out the bitch in me. "I can't believe she gave her husband my pussy" I blurted out as I looked over to see my homeboy looking at me crazy. In that moment I realized how ridiculous I sounded and instantly felt ashamed. How could I let myself get to this point I thought as I struggle to contain my emotions? It took another couple of days for the realization to set in that I was just a little side dick; some "feel good" for her during a down period in her marriage. The Captain Save-A-Hoe cape did not fit me well, unfortunately it wouldn't be the last time I would wear it. Ultimately nothing made me feel better but time.

Years later I'd be on a steady routine of cycling women in and out of my life every couple months when my best friend would tell me he wanted me to go on a double date with him. As a good homeboy should he gave me a good wingman opportunity with one of his chick's sisters. I think her being from Maryland too was a reason he thought it might be a good connection. We got to a local restaurant before them so we grabbed a table and waited. Before long two fine thick ass women came walking in as my friend nodded to them. He introduced us as I tried my best to hold my excitement and anxiety in as we spoke to each other. She had to be at least 5'9"- 5'10", medium brown skinned, pretty smile, dimples, nice breast & a big ole booty. She wasn't a fat chick so not fat girl big booty but sit a drink on it thick girl big booty, by far the baddest woman I've ever dealt with. The date went really good, we hit it off she was more down to earth than I was expecting.

All that badness came at a cost though but one I was willing to pay because I'd paid it before, she had 4 kids so if we got serious back into stepdaddy mode I would go. Still not sure if there's something about single mothers with several children that attracts me to them or something about me that attracts women with a lot of kids to me, either way kids are usually never the issue. Anyway we exchanged numbers and went on a few dates of our own. We bonded over trauma, she'd tell me some of the things she went through in her life mostly childhood trauma and I'd tell her mine. Knowing this sparked the protector in me so I wanted to save her and the children from the instability and potential drama for a lessor man. I may be a lot of things but I'm not a bad man, I'm a really good man actually. My methods and ways of communicating may turn people off by my intentions are never malicious. I wasn't pussy whipped because the sex really wasn't good, due to certain traumatic experiences she didn't like rough sex or intense sex. She liked it more slow and deliberate which I wasn't necessarily accustomed to. I wanted her enough to do my best to learn her way of being intimate and I did at least once.

She had some business to handle in Maryland and she asked me if I could take her. I love to drive and I thought it would be a nice road trip, 12 hour drive each way didn't deter me my nose was wide open. We talked, laughed and vibed to 90's music since we're both 80's babies. Even as I write this I have a big grin on my face because even the memories bring the joyful feeling of the experience. An even better feeling would come the night after we arrived. I would consider one of the only true love making sessions I've ever had. We kissed, licked, rubbed, stroked you name it as far as foreplay we did it. I ended up standing next to the bed with her on all fours in front of me giving her slow, deliberate strokes while firmly gripping that big ass booty. I added a grind at the end of every stroke to make sure she got everything I had to give. That's a fat nigga tip for all my big fellas, thank me later. Out of nowhere the bottom of both of me feet started to tingle, that feeling shot up both my legs, back and neck. I swear I saw stars, I've heard about male orgasms and this had to be it. I don't remember anything else that night after that.

After that I thought I'd be wrapped around her finger for life. In a way I felt like a crackhead chasing that first high but no matter how many times I tried with her or other women after her I've yet to feel it again. Ultimately that experience taught me the significance of our emotions and mental connections in the realm of sex. I can't remember if we were in a relationship before the trip but after that experience we definitely were. I vaguely remember disagreements about possible business ventures for her, money management and somewhat crucial topics that have a big impact on building family. I was driving trucks over the road so I wasn't home a lot, so our relationship was grounded in conversation. So when that started going sour so did my feelings for her. I kept my own place but I stayed with her a lot and I let her drive my car while I was away and I helped financially when needed. Things began to look one-sided to me, I never got the tingly feeling anymore and our conversations were mostly debates.

After a lot of internal back and forth I decided to end the relationship because at that point is more draining than anything beneficial for me and I didn't see a good ending. It hurt her too, I can't speak for her to say how much but she refused to bring my car to me. She left the keys in her mailbox one day and told me I could pick it up while she was gone. I remember thinking "Damn are you really going to dump the finest woman you've ever had?", I had to for my own sanity. I still loved her though and I wished the best for her. I would look her up on social media for any new pictures every so often, maybe even send her a message. Sometimes she would respond other times she'd ignore or block me. I'm sure it was due to her dealing with a guy which I wasn't angry I understood how things go. A few years pass when I get a message from her telling me she's in a bind and needs a ride to a bus station in Tennessee. I knew she was in a relationship so of course I asked her why her man couldn't do it.

She insinuated that they were on the brink of breaking up which satisfied my ego enough that I thought about helping. "When do you need to go?" I asked as she shot a text back quickly "NOW!!!", my antennas are up now because this seems like an emergency. Nobody ups and catches a bus from a station four hours away with 4 kids. "Aite" I said as I rolled out of bed to get dressed, lucky for her she caught me on my home time. It was early afternoon already so I knew I had to get going so I could be back home at a decent hour because it was an 8 hour drive there and back. I pulled up to a house I assume where she was staying and watched as she and her kids loaded my car with bags. "Yea I'm driving 8 hours, I ain't helping carrying no damn bags" I thought as to soothe my feeling of being used. I didn't mind though, I still loved her and it was obvious she needed me in that moment. They finished loading up and we rolled out, the ride was smooth they fell asleep for the most part. After buying the kids something to eat from a fast food restaurant Shelly and I talked a little but not much. I didn't want her to feel any worse about her situation or possibly shame from telling me what was really going on.

I actually enjoyed watching them sleep, when we arrived I helped unload their bags and slipped her a little money, told her to be safe and the let me know when they made it to where they were going. She messaged me maybe a day or so later letting me know they were safe and communication went silent again after that. Maybe another year or 2 went by before another message comes through from her. Starting out with a simple "Hey how are you?" turned into a conversation about borrowing money. It's pretty clear she's using me when it suits her at this point and I should've said "No" but I didn't. She asked if I could meet her at a local restaurant where she was having lunch after church with family. All I could think about on the way there was how I could try to reconnect with her so I could fuck her again. The only pleasant thing about the exchange was pulling up seeing some leather pants hugging that big ass of hers. The parking lot was full so I pulled up to her and rolled my window down. I could see in her eyes she had no interest in carrying a casual conversation with me so I gave her the money, she said she'd pay me back in a couple weeks and we said our goodbyes.

As you can imagine I never got my money back. I messaged her a few months later asking about it, really just wanting to start a conversation with her. To my surprise she blocked me and that was the end of that or so I thought. I felt real lame for allowing myself to be used all in the name of getting some ass again. Especially from a chick that I dumped, I guess I got what I deserved. It did harden me up a bit to the women I dealt with after that situation. Another two years or so passed before I found myself unblocked and being messaged by her again. "What this bitch want now?" I thought to myself as I opened the message. Her line of questioning was a bit different this time. "Where are you?", "Are you single?" were the questions she was asking which excited me because it sounded like she wanted to fuck this time. Sure enough that's where the conversation led, we made plans for later that night. I'd been waiting for this moment since soon after I dumped her and it was finally here. "Here's my chance to get the tingly feet again" I said to myself as I awaited her arrival.

The doorbell ringing was music to my ears, I made my way to the door anticipating the sight of her. She stepped inside soon after I opened the door to greet me with a hug and smile. I immediately notice her nipples poking through her shirt, titties and ass were bigger more than likely from the child she had since I last saw her. After my initial lustful survey of her body I noticed pain in her eyes, she hid it well physically but I was still connected to her enough to notice. I didn't want to ruin the mood, a part of me figured I could fuck some happiness into her. We made casual conversation as we made our way to my room that already had low lights, lit candles and soft music playing. She immediately stripped down to a pink bra/panties set and got into bed. I was already in bed completely naked ready for the foreplay. Her kisses and touches were all cold, literally and figuratively. This was a moment I'd been waiting for so I tried to ignore her obvious disinterest and enjoy the moment. "You want me to suck your dick?" she asked which was odd because that was a no brainer. "Yea" I whispered as she went down on me, even that wasn't enjoyable she was just going through the motions. I laid her down and mounted her after giving her some head, she was aroused a bit but by the time we got to doggystyle her coochie was dry.

After a minute or so in that position I faked a nut to end things, I'm sure she knows I faked it because as dry as she was she would've felt it. We pillow talked for a few before she told me she had to get back to her kids. The little desire I had for her was finally gone but I still questioned why she came over in the 1st place. After thinking on it all night and the next day it was obvious to me somebody broke her heart. Calling me up was a desperate search to connect to someone or something. I know because most of my 20's I did the same thing. At least she can cross my name of the list of possible solutions to her emotional issues at that time I hoped. Even though the desire is gone she'll always hold a tender spot in my heart and on my dick.

My Lady

One day during the summer of my 12th birthday I noticed a black cat lounging around a corner store on my block, I started sharing my food and snacks with her. After a few days I asked my mother if I could bring her home and she agreed. I used food to lure her in of course, "Lady" is what I named her. She was a black short haired cat with lots of healed scars, she had obviously been in plenty of fights. One problem though, she was moody as fuck; most days she would bite and scratch me if I tried to pick her up without feeding her. In my mind she was traumatized and didn't know how to receive love. I figured if I just love up on her enough she would see I wasn't there to hurt her and let me take care of her. So everyday I'd pick her up and pet her as she bit and scratched me continuously. Did it hurt? Of course but I felt more sadness for her and whatever she was going through emotionally. I know it sounds crazy I'm talking about an animal this way but that's the emotional relationship I had with her. After a while my mother noticed my scars and told me I was a dumb ass and to put the cat out. I did but still wondered if she was ok for weeks afterwards, little did I know that experience would be a subconscious template for relationships to come. One however stands out from the rest and has become a permanent part of my life's highlight reel.

One random day back in 2013 I got a phone call from one of my cousins asking if I could be in his wedding, of course I said yes. Up until that point no one in our family had an actual wedding so I was excited to be a part of it. Maybe a week or so later his fiancée called telling me she paired me with a friend of hers because we were the tallest man & woman in the wedding party. She asked if she could exchange our numbers so we could get familiar with each other before the wedding; I definitely didn't have a problem with that. I can't remember who text 1st but our conversations were short and dry for a couple of weeks. One day she gave me enough attention to actually ask questions and really started getting to know me. When she found out we were born 2 days apart in the same year she really opened up to me. I can't remember much about those conversations other than she had a dry, sarcastic humor just like me. She reminded me of a female version of myself, we would even finish each other's sentences sometimes. I couldn't wait to meet her, my anticipation of physically meeting the woman I'd been spending so much time talking to for the past few months was through the roof.

I traveled up to D.C. where the wedding would take place a day or 2 earlier to hang out with her. She was equally excited because she suggested I stay with her instead of getting a hotel room. "I'm outside", I text her as I drove up and down her crowded block to find a parking spot. Once parked I took my suitcase out the trunk and waited leaning against my car. The door to her apartment building swung open as she lightly jogged to me full of enthusiasm wearing a big smile. I instantly got butterflies and my heart was racing, I developed feelings for her just from our phone conversations but this solidified it; this was love at 1st sight. She was 6' tall, thick, full lips & her glasses complemented her cheeks perfectly. Before I could gather my words she wrapped her arms around me and told me how glad she was that I made it. "I'm doing my homegirl's hair but I'm almost done", she said as we walked back to her place. We walk in to her friend sitting in a chair only half braided. She said I could lay down in her room but I told her I was fine with sitting with them and waiting.

I chuckled inside because the braids she did after my arrival looked terrible. She was clearly rushing to get her homegirl out of there. After they were done we talked a little and decided to call it a night, I stripped down to my underwear and I believe she wore a T-shirt. We lay next to each other and the attraction is obviously strong but so is the anxiety. I'm running scenarios through my head but they get washed away by the thought of rejection so I decide to go to sleep. I rolled over to go to sleep, immediately after she rolled over and uttered, "you going to sleep?" That was all the confirmation I needed that we wanted the same thing. I entered her from back as we spooned and we were inseparable after that or so I thought. A few months went by of mostly phone conversations because I drove trucks at the time. Our Birthdays were approaching so we decided to spend them together. I took notice to certain brands she wore like Dooney & Bourke & Tory Burch so I bought her a couple purses, a pair of Tory Burch flats I saw her admiring online one day, a swatch watch to replace the one she wore all the time & she fancied Godiva chocolate so I bought her a chocolate tower gift set. I also booked a nice room in Ocean City, MD with a jacuzzi facing fire place & a dinner reservation at Ruth's Chris. As you can probably tell my nose was wide open, I was in love with her and wanted to make this a memorable weekend.

I arrived to D.C. on my birthday, parked my truck and rented a car because she was still at work. I visited family and friends in Baltimore to kill some time before meeting at her place. Her energy was different now, she didn't seem too excited to see me & conversation was dry and short. She gave me a few polo t-shirts and an ugly pair of polo shoes that were obviously not my style, she didn't put any thought into my gifts and it hurt my feelings a little. It had been at least a month since we last saw each other so I wanted sex obviously. We watched a little T.V. in her living room before I decided to lay in her bed hoping she'd join me. She never did and my excitement slowly started to fade, especially after I asked if she would join me to which she replied , "No I'm good". Coincidentally a chapter of my car club at the time were hanging out at a restaurant not too far from us and invited me out. I asked her to join me and of course she declined again. I decided to go alone, feeling miserable not getting any attention or affection on my birthday didn't sit well with me. I'm not a drinker but I had a few and the more I drank the more resentment built up for her. "I'm going through all this planning for her birthday and this is how she does me for mine? I thought while changing my mind about driving the 3 hours to Ocean City to set up our room before driving back to pick her up from work the following day.

Once I sobered up enough to drive to her place I did so, with the same resenting thoughts flowing through my mind. I decided to give her gifts to her that night so I carried the big box I had with everything in it up to her apartment. After she let me in she sat back on the couch, "Happy Birthday" I rambled out as I threw the box onto the floor close to where she sat.

I went directly to her room and went to bed, didn't wait for her to look at anything or give any response. The next day I didn't take the excessive drive I just waited for her to get off work and we took the drive together. Once we got in the room she finally blessed me with some coochie so that lightened my mood. I gave her four hundred dollars as pocket change & I told her I was taking her shopping the next day at the nearby outlet mall. The next day was her birthday and we had a day full of shopping, walking the boardwalk & enjoying each other's company. That night we changed for dinner & got to the restaurant in time for our 8 o'clock reservation.

We both scrolled social media while waiting for our food; I came across a photo of the menu she just posted that with a caption that read "It's no Cheesecake Factory but it'll do". It felt like a slap in the face and my mood started to shift after reading that, we're at an upscale steakhouse & she's downing if for the cheesecake factory. "I'm sick of this ungrateful bitch" I thought while trying not to let my emotions fuck up the night. In the midst of our conversation she tells me we can't stay up late because we have to get up early to head back because she's throwing herself a birthday cookout. I was bit frustrated but I didn't argue much, plus I was almost certain it was a joint birthday party for the both of us since our birthdays were so close and she knew I had never had a birthday party in my life. We got back early the next morning around 4am and went back to sleep. I woke up to her getting ready to move the party items to a local park with one of her friends, she told me I could rest a little longer which further heightened my expectations of a surprise for me. That was short lived when I decided to take a peek at the cake that was left behind, surely it had both of our names on it. As you can imagine I was wrong, just her name in her favorite color. My feelings were hurt and I played back everything I did and considered for her birthday versus what she did and considered for mine and it didn't add up by a long shot. "I'm outta here" I thought as I packed my bags, she came back to grab more supplies as I loaded the last of my bags into my rental car. "You leaving?" she yelled to me from across the street; "Yea" I replied. "Ok" she uttered so nonchalantly it almost brought tears to my eyes, I got in the car and left.

We didn't talk for a few months, it was over as far as I was concerned or so I thought. I had gotten into a situationship with a beautiful soft spoken woman from Tennessee. I visited her for the most part, she came to visit me a time or 2. Things were good; unfortunately I wasn't use to "good" so my toxic nature picked things to critique about her. Like my daughter's mother I took her submissive nature as a weakness and I agitated meaningless conflict. She never indulged though, she would just give me the silent treatment. One day a mutual family friend called me shortly after I posted Christmas photos of my new boo & I on social media. "Lady wants to talk to you, she misses you" she said as I smirked while telling her she could give her my new phone number. Not long after I ended up at her place around new years eve, she knew I was in a relationship but she didn't care. I didn't either, I knew my heart was still with her so my conscience was absent that night. I felt bad the next day, not a regretful for cheating bad but a "I should have never gotten this new woman involved" bad. I was still trucking then so my next route was going directly to my woman's city and I made up my mind I was going to tell her and break up. It was only right to not string her along anymore, I know it sounds really fucked up to break up with someone after you cheated but that's what I did. She was pissed obviously and probably wouldn't speak to me till this day.

After a few months Lady & I decided she would move down to alabama with me to start a life together. At that point I was a rolling stone, I lived in my truck and had all of my possessions in storage. So I found a nice gated apartment complex for us, besides my daughter she was the most important person to me so I wanted her safe and comfortable. She found a job in the area and things were good for about 3 weeks or so. One day I lay across our bed while she braided my daughter's hair in the living room, a notification bell came from her phone that lay next to me on her side of the bed. Until that moment I didn't realize her phone was in the room, I ignored and gazed back toward the ceiling burying myself in thought about life and my plans. Another notification came through breaking my concentration again, "It might be something important, I'll just take it to her" I thought as I picked up her phone and started getting up from the bed. "Fat Mafucka" caught my attention when I glanced at her phone, then I noticed it was from an unsaved number so I was curious enough to read the messages. Those messages turned out to be from her ex-boyfriend, he was asking her why did she move down south with a "Fat Mafucka" and basically hating on me and our relationship. All her previous messages were telling him that they could still be friends and that she moved down to go to school or some bullshit like that. O I was crushed reading that, not only did she not defend me at all but she didn't acknowledge that she moved down to start a new life with me. I got so angry I could barely see straight and mild headache came from out of nowhere.

My new life as I knew it came crashing down, "stay calm nigga, at least in front of baby girl" I thought as I decided if I would address this now or later. "Fuck that, I ain't waiting" I thought as I walked into the living room and asked Lady to talk to me in our 2nd Bathroom which was closer to her. She wore a confused look as she walked to the bathroom because I'm sure my face told that I was pissed. I had never been that angry in my life and definitely not with her. I can't remember what I said I just remember I yelled so loud I could see saliva flying from my mouth and a scared look on her face every so often when my vison cleared in between sentences because the vibration of my voice shook my head so much it blurred my vision. I was angry but more so hurt that the woman I spent most of my days thinking about how best to take care of was entertaining a dude who didn't or couldn't offer her what I knew I could. A few moments later I decided to take my daughter home to her mother, I didn't want her to hear me like that anymore than she already had. By the time I got back Lady was gone. Her stuff was still there so I know she didn't leave for good, I found out after I got back on the road a couple days later that she stayed at a hotel until I was gone. She said I scared her, that made me feel like a monster even though I felt justified in voicing my frustrations. She apologized for talking to him, still didn't see an issue with them being "friends" but told me she would cut him off completely. I came home maybe a week or so later, we had more conversations about that situation and how we felt. We laughed, cried and made love so I thought everything was good and that we had made up.

I left again and came back about 2 weeks later, the whole time we'd been talking regularly so I wasn't alarmed by anything. She didn't answer her phone when I called so that she could pick me up from my truck which I parked about a mile or so from our apartment. It was the middle of the day on a Saturday so I knew she wasn't at work. I grabbed my bags and began that mile walk home, "What if I walk in and she's fucking somebody" I thought, I contemplated who I would kill 1st and how I would do it. Then I thought about the possibility of her being hurt and in the hospital, either way my anxiety was through the roof. I got home to find a cutoff notice for the electricity on the door, that was her only bill she was responsible for. Once I saw that I knew she wasn't there, going in validated what I already knew; she left me. Immediately a gut wrenching, empty feeling came over me & a subconscious sense of abandonment. She didn't answer my phone calls for a couple weeks, apparently fear fueled her exit. "You scared me, I thought you were going to hit me." She said, I definitely disagreed but I respected her feelings. I didn't respect her not being honest with me and leading me to believe that we made up before I left prior to her leaving. I had to get over it though because maybe a month or so later she told me she was pregnant, Deja Fuckin Vu right? With baby #2 on the way I swallowed my pride and anger about the situation to be cordial with her. Shortly after we planned on her flying down to visit as part of a plan to ultimately get back together.

She came down and we had a pretty good time up until she asked if I was dealing with any women. "Of Course" I responded, I didn't understand why she would think any different. My response infuriated her; she just happened to be in my kitchen so she grabbed a coffee mug and slammed it in the trash can. It didn't stop there, after she smashed every mug into the garbage she moved on to the plates. "You won't be feeding bitches with the plates that I bought." She yelled angrily while smashing them with the rest of my dishes. I just sat there and let her get her anger out, "I wonder if she realizes she bought those dishes with my money so technically they're mine" I thought but I didn't say a word. I figured she didn't give a fuck either way, as long as she didn't throw any at me I was relatively unbothered. She had some nerve to leave me and expect me to mope around until she decided if she wanted to come back; especially when it was her disrespect or lack of respect that triggered the entire conflict. "Take me to the airport" she said after breaking the last dish, "Your flight doesn't leave for like 3 hours" I replied. "I don't give a fuck, I want to go" she retorted, without much hesitation I took her to the airport and hoped she would make it back without incident. Months later she would tell me her flight was delayed a couple hours so she sat in the airport for a total of 5 hours, that amused me that her stubbornness had her sit there instead of calling me to come get her.

She had our oldest son shortly after and as you can imagine having a newborn stirred up feelings of wanting to be a family. This time I was determined to get it right, I started off visiting her and our son as often as possible; knocked her up again so baby #3 was en route. There was still some uncertainty because of how many times she'd left me before so I took advantage of us not officially being in a relationship. There was a woman I'd been talking to on and off for at least 6 years but we never had any physical contact. One weekend our schedules and vibe matched up and we had sex for the 1st and last time. She had a big ass booty and her head was good but she gave off deceptive energy so I told myself to stay away from her. Maybe a month before my lady moved back down to Alabama the "fling" told me she was pregnant , my stomach instantly turned. Of course I wasn't excited about the news and that infuriated her, she went from talking about making my life a living hell to getting an abortion. She was all over the place with her moods so I stopped talking to her after I told her I'd pay for the abortion. There was no way in hell I was going to tell Lady about this "ghetto twin" situation, we just got things ironed out. I was closing on a house as soon as she made it back and the fantasy of a wife, kids and home in a nice suburban area was finally on the cusp of coming into fruition.

When "Lady" made it down I closed on our house, I bought her an SUV and I bought myself a big rig as I was transitioning into my own trucking business; Life was perfect. After Lady and I got settled in we went to eat at my favorite steakhouse when the universe decided to shake things up a bit. As we sat at an open table in the middle of the restaurant I noticed an old black woman sitting in my line of sight a couple tables behind lady; she kept staring at us. Finally she got up and made her way to us, "Ya'll look like a beautiful couple, GOD gave me a message; I don't know which one of ya'll it's for." She said with confidence. I took a sip of my tea preparing to hear some religious mumbo jumbo. "He's about to put something back in your life that was taken but you have a choice to make and it must be the righteous one." As she shifted her eyes and body language between the both of us. My heart started beating out my chest as I tried not to wear guilt on my face because I instantly thought about the fling pregnancy. I looked at Lady as she looked back at me confused, "You're being blessed but it'll only continue if you do the righteous thing." She uttered as she walked back to her table. I cracked a smile, shook my head and thought about how I was going to break the news to Lady. Certainly not in this restaurant I thought, if she's going to hit me I'd rather get punched in the car.

I felt like a child waiting for daddy to come home after I got suspended, the nervousness was something I haven't felt since my childhood. Once we got in the car I couldn't hold it in any longer as she brought up the old lady and what she said. "It was for me I have something to tell you. A few months before you came down I had sex with someone and she's pregnant." I blurted out as I braced for impact. "Who is she? What's her name?" Lady asked, "a chick I'd been talking to online for years , I only know her 1st name." I replied. "Really Nigga?" she shot back with disappointment in her eyes. I told her she planned on having an abortion and I'd be paying for it, she responded with an "Ok" and didn't say much to me for most of the ride home. As I pulled in our subdivision she put her phone in my face and asked "Is this the bitch?" she asked; it definitely was and I don't know how she found her because I wasn't even able to find her on facebook. I confirmed her identity and we wouldn't speak of it much until abortion time rolled around and I called the clinic to make the payment as Lady and I stood in our kitchen. It was a relief for me but I still wondered if Lady was truly as ok as she made it seem.

I tried to be as attentive to her as I could be, I'd watch home remodeling shows because that seemed to be her favorite so I'd have something of interest to her to talk about. She said she wanted to work, then she said she wanted to be a stay-at-home mom. I supported every decision she chose and still she didn't seem to be happy. On one of my home time breaks from trucking I thought it would do us some good to have a family day. I told her the day prior that the following day I wanted everyone to turn off their electronics. I wanted to spend a day as a family with little distraction. "We can take the kids to the playground, play board games, get ice cream or even go to the movie theater." I said with excited anticipation written all over my face. "That sounds good" she replied, I didn't have much of a plan but I knew it would be a great day because I've never experienced a family day not even in my own childhood. The next morning I wake up to multiple TV's on, kids on tablets, she's on her phone, I immediately felt disappointed. I didn't tell anyone to turn anything off I just laid there in defeat. I noticed no one was watching the TV in our room so I told her to turn that television off at least. That might as well been a lit fuse to a stick of dynamite, she gets up and goes off on me. I honestly don't remember everything she said only her pointing out that my phone was on, even though I needed it on to conduct business she didn't care. She also kept complaining about the puppy I had gotten us so I decided to give him away to a friend.

I got dressed and took the dog to my friend's house where I stayed for maybe an hour or 2 just talking and cooling off. I pull back in my garage to find her car gone so I figured she'd went to the grocery store or something. Until I went inside the house and noticed decorations gone and rooms ravaged with obvious clothes and other belongings gone. She'd left me again, my stomach was in knots and my calls and texts to her went unanswered. My last message to her that day was asking her to return my credit card, which was just a way to get her back so we could talk. I spent that day replaying everything in my mind wondering what I did wrong and frustration set in when I couldn't figure it out. Later that night I randomly got a call from the crazy Tennessee chick I use to mess with asking if I was home because she wanted to come by after she left the club. Sex was my favorite way to get over heartbreak so I agreed. Just like that I was getting my dick sucked by another woman the same day Lady left. My heart started racing when a text popped up on my phone that read "Your Card is in the mailbox". Lucky for me I had chick park in my garage and Lady didn't decide to come in because she still had a key.

After my guest left I went back to feeling the pain of being abandoned yet again. I felt like a failure not only to myself but my 2 sons we share. They wouldn't get to grow up in a home with both parents, I knew something would lack within them If I wasn't around enough. Her moving back to D.C. there was no way I'd be able to be in their life as much as I wanted or they needed. Suicidal thoughts soon consumed my mind, irrational thoughts of how I might be more valuable to them dead. Drugs? No I tried that before unsuccessfully, blowing my brains out would be the most guaranteed way to go I thought. I grabbed my .45 caliber Glock 41 loaded a round in the chamber and sat on the edge of my bed. I cried as I replayed my life's highlight reel in my mind which was full of trauma & disappointment. In that moment the hairs stood up on the back of my neck and my arms. I felt pressure on both of my forearms as if I was being touched as a familiar calm and comfort came over me. The same calm and comfort I felt hiding under my grandmother's hospice bed. It had to be her I thought as I interpreted the experience as a sign that I was about to make a major mistake. I released the magazine, pulled the slide to eject the round from the chamber and never touched that gun again until I sold it.

A couple months passed before Lady cooled down enough to talk to me about anything outside of our kids. I don't know if it was genuine love, a toxic pattern or both but we started to hit it off again. Like our usual disagreements once she'd calmed down I'd explain to her what was actually said and done opposed to what she felt was said and done. At which point she'd admit fault and apologize, even knowing she could leave me at any moment I wanted her back. I knew she had what I wanted and needed she just couldn't be consistent. I thought if I kept loving on her one day we'd stick and she'd realize with me was the best place for her to be and I'd be satisfied seeing her fulfilled. She moved back a few months later and we were back on course, for the time being at least. I tried connecting her with some local women to hang out with and got her a bike with a carriage attached for the kids so she could take rides. I knew sitting at home with nothing to do would cause the same issues and I communicated my concern with her, she assured me it wouldn't.

As for me I was stressed out dealing with running a business and maintaining a home. Owning a big rig is no simple task, a breakdown could cost a couple thousand dollars at least and mine broke down almost regularly. Due to her mishaps earlier on with money management and keeping up with due dates I decided managing bills would be my responsibility. Between business and home I had 13 different bills to keep track of and it started to wear down on me mentally. I'd love to just put money in an account and trust she'd make sure things were paid but I didn't have that faith in her. Depression started creeping up on me again which for me shows as emotional eating and excessive sleeping. "Can you talk to me while I walk? I want to walk for at least 20 minutes every day to get some kind of exercise." I asked to which she replied "Yes". That lasted for one walk, her conversation was dry, short and I felt like I was inconveniencing her at best. Instead of the walk and conversation making me feel better it made me feel worse and I dove deeper into depression. I still kept my poker face on though. When business was crappy and money was short I made sure to send as much as I could to her even if it meant not eating for a day or two. No need to tell her I thought because it was my responsibility as the man of our family.

Instead when I came home I was met with complaints about what she doesn't have or what I didn't do and how I needed to give her a break from the kids. I pushed back some because we had a babysitter on call if she ever wanted to have some time to herself. Still I'd tell her to have some alone time when I got home even coordinating with the babysitter so we could have a date night. Maybe it was the depression but I felt like I would die soon and my family didn't have any financial security which lead to more frustration. One day as she was doing her hair in the bathroom I thought I'd proposition with the only security I could offer. "I was thinking about signing majority ownership of my company over to you. If something happens to me you could hire a driver, run the truck and make money." I said. "I don't want to be in the trucking business." She said, I fought letting the rejection overcome my emotions as I tried to reason with her. It turned into a slight argument to which I left the room because I couldn't understand how trying to offer her some financial security turned into an argument.

The miserable days grew more frequent with every visit home, it seemed like after a day or so she'd be upset about something. No sex, No food, No loving environment only thing I was guaranteed at home was tension. I stayed in bed most of the time because my desire to do anything was gone due to the rejection of almost every idea I had from movie nights to family days. One day after taking a shower at a Truck Stop I noticed holes in my underwear as I got dressed. Then a toe slipped through a hole in my socks, "I make too much money for this shit." I thought as I continued to get dressed. For the next few days I would think of me and lady's relationship and I wondered why she never thought to buy me new underclothes because she did do my laundry when I came home. Maybe it's my fault but all I could think of was her and our kids, making sure she had extra money to take trips home or getting the kids horse riding lessons. With all the consideration I give some new underclothes would've made me feel respected. As you can imagine a man feeling disrespected in his home will not end well.

I came home one day to instant attitude, I can't remember what she was upset about. I just knew I wouldn't be getting any sex and she told me to make my own dinner plate. Before I could get up I got a text, "I made chicken tonight, you want some." From an old fling who I stayed cordial with over the years. So instead of making my own plate I drove 20 minutes to her house where she fed and fucked me. I got home at exactly midnight, I know because Lady's alarm went of as I walked into our room so I looked at the time. She didn't say anything, I already washed up before I left ole girl's house so I got straight in bed and went to sleep. A couple hours later she started grinding on me which I knew was her queue to have sex. It took me by surprise because she usually doesn't want to have sex when she was upset. I wasn't ashamed at what I had done because it technically wasn't cheating because she agreed to a polygynous relationship but that moment was a horrible time to tell her. So I kept my mouth shut and handled my business. Afterwards I felt extremely vulnerable and wanted to tell her about what I've been dealing with emotionally but I know it didn't come out in the most productive way possible.

"I feel like you're killing me" I uttered to which she replied "I guess I'll leave then". Those words stung and I let her know immediately, "that being the 1st thing that comes to mind shows that you don't want to be here." I said as she rejected that idea. I pointed out how she loved interior design but be have an almost 3,000 sqft. home that isn't decorated at all. She blamed me for not giving her enough money to decorate which was complete bullshit so the conversation fizzled out and we went back to sleep. Later that morning she went grocery shopping and came back as I was getting dressed to get back on the road. I guess her thoughts wandered as she shopped because she came straight to me as soon as she returned how. "Did you fuck somebody last night?" she blurted out as I put on a shirt. "Yes I did" I replied. "And came back and fucked me?" she shot back, I knew it would sound fucked up but it was the truth; "I washed off" I said. Her eyes were so full of rage but she knew hitting me would probably result in a fight, I don't believe in being anyone's punching bag especially not a 6' 300lbs woman.

She stormed out of the room and finished putting the groceries away. After that she took me to my truck as I expressed all of my grievances. It all seemed to go in one ear and out the other, "I don't have everything I want" She shouted. "Like what?" I asked to which she replied "I don't have money to get my nails done." She said. "So I'm supposed to keep track of all the bills, give you a break when I come home, help you find some purpose and I'm supposed to schedule your nail appointments? What the fuck do I need you for if I have to do everything" I said angrily. She didn't have a response, probably because she knew that was a bullshit excuse because she had enough money and I would've given her anything she asked for. I grew angrier because my entire existence at that point was centered around giving her and our kids the most comfortable life possible so to say something lacked I felt unappreciated. "What do you do for me?" I asked, "I guess nothing" she shot back. Sarcastically of course but the reality is for whatever reason the woman that use to brush my beard, wipe my sweat and fix my clothes out in public was gone. I did however realize that being in the relationship hurt more than her absence when we broke up.

When I came home again I told her it was best if we broke up but I wanted to be friends, "We can never be friends" she replied. She also turned down my offer to help her get on her feet in Alabama instead of going back to D.C. We set a timeline for a few months out, she wanted to get things in order to move back. She asked if I could give her money to visit D.C. for her sister's graduation, she asked for $1000 I gave her $1500 and told her I'd send more in a week when I got paid. Unfortunately my big rig broke down again and I had to spend my check on the repair. She was everything but understanding and cursed me out, I was so disgusted I told her to stay in D.C. and I'd send the rest of her things when I could. That was the end of my longest relationship and just like the cat I had to let go of something I loved dearly even though it brought me pain. She'll always be MY LADY.

Milton Keynes UK
Ingram Content Group UK Ltd.
UKHW020217050924
447823UK00011B/505

9 798218 485351